Preface
to Luke

Preface
to Luke

by
Harold Riley

PEETERS　　　**MERCER**

ISBN 0-86554-423-9 MUP/H337

Preface to Luke
Copyright ©1993
Mercer University Press, Macon, Georgia 31207 USA
All rights reserved
Printed in the United States of America

The paper used in this publication meets the minimum requirements
of American National Standard for Informtion Services—
Permanence of Paper for Printed Library Materials, ANSI Z39.48–1984.

Library of Congress Cataloging-in-Publication Data
Riley, Harold.
Preface to Luke / by Harold Riley.
viii+148 pages. 6x9" (15x23cm.).
Includes bibliographical references and indexes.
ISBN 0-86554-423-9 (hbk : alk. paper)
1. Bible. N.T. Luke 1:1-4—Criticism, interpretation, etc.
I. Title.
BS2595.2.R54   1993   93-18721
226.4'06—dc20   CIP

Contents

Dedication

To

James P. S. Thomson
DM (Lambeth), MS, FRCS

with admiration and gratitude

Preface

Many recent studies have been concerned with the theology of the Gospels, and particularly that of St. Luke. The conclusions reached depend on the assessments made—and sometimes on the assumptions made—of the relation of Luke to other writings in the New Testament, and concerning the sources the author used. Among such studies are works of great erudition that have behind them two assumptions. The first, following what was almost unchallenged critical orthodoxy before the publication of Farmer's book *The Synoptic Problem*, is that Mark is the earliest of the Gospels and a major source of the other two Synoptists. With Farmer, I believe it can be shown that Mark is in fact a conflation of material from Matthew and Luke, and in particular that Matthew, not Mark, is the one extant source used by Luke.

From a study of the internal evidence of the text, I have set out the general evidence for this in part 1 of *The Order of the Synoptics* (by Bernard Orchard and Harold Riley, Mercer, 1987), and from a more detailed study of St. Mark's Gospel in *The Making of Mark* (Mercer, 1989). In the latter, I argued that the text of Matthew available to Mark was shorter than that of the canonical Gospels. This was followed up in *The First Gospel* (1992), in which I argued that a shorter text—for which the name Proto-Matthew may be used, can be distinguished from the later edited text, and that it was this shorter text that was available not only to Mark but to Luke also. Evidence for this, from a consideration of the contents, method, and order of the Third Gospel, is a major part of the subject matter of the present book.

A second general assumption of Luke studies is that the Third Gospel and Acts belong to the postapostolic period, and that the traditional ascription of their authorship to Luke, Paul's traveling companion, is untenable. On the contrary, I believe there is overwhelming evidence to support the traditional ascription of authorship, and a correspondingly early date, and have sought here to show its validity.

If these judgments are right, there is need to reconsider much that has been written about Luke's theology, as about other matters relating to the Gospels. But this is outside the scope of the present study, which really asks one simple question: What are the implications of the first sentence of the Third Gospel, the "preface to Luke"?

Biblical quotations are in general from the (English) Revised Version (1881–1889), as being a more literal translation than later versions, and therefore more convenient in the comparison of different passages, but I have varied from it when to do so has made for greater clarity.

Abbreviations

ASV	American Standard Version (Standard American Edition of the Revised Version of the Bible, 1901)
ERV or RV	English Revised Version (1881–1889)
NEB	New English Bible (1961, 1970)
NRSV	New Revised Standard Version (1990)
REB	Revised English Bible (1989)
RSV	Revised Standard Version (1946, 1952, 1957, NT^{2}1971)

Chapter 1

The Preface to the Gospel

Forasmuch as many have taken in hand to draw up a narrative concerning those matters which have been fulfilled among us, even as they delivered them unto us, which were from the beginning eyewitnesses and ministers of the word, it seemed good to me also, having traced the course of all things accurately from the first, to write unto thee in order, most excellent Theophilus, that thou mightest know the certainty concerning the things wherein thou wast instructed.

—Luke 1:1-4

In their different ways, three of the Evangelists specify the purpose for which they have written. Mark does so concisely with his opening words: "The beginning of the Gospel of Jesus Christ, the Son of God" (Mark 1:1). John, in what (apart from the appendix of chapter 21) are his final words: "these are written that ye may believe that Jesus is the Christ, the Son of God; and that believing ye may have life in his name" (John 20:31). Luke does so more fully, both in the closely knit preface to his Gospel (1:1-4) and, more diffusely, looking back to his Gospel and forward to its continuation, in the first eight verses of Acts. Together these two statements of Luke provide a key to Luke's understanding of his task in his "two-volume" work.

The convention Luke followed in writing the prefatory words that begin his two volumes and the formal dedication to Theophilus are indications of the use he expected to be made of them. Whereas Matthew's Gospel appears to have been compiled precisely to be read in the Christian assemblies, it is not likely that Luke, writing such words, expected his book to be so used; or for that matter that he would expect a work like his—the kind of material included, much of it reported in the first person—to be put to such use. Luke was writing a book for a reading public, though doubtless a limited one, of whom Theophilus was a representative. There are indications indeed that it took longer for Luke's first volume than for Matthew to be adopted as a church book—as one of "the Gospels." It was to explain to his prospective readers why he had written, and to give the formal introduction appropriate with such a readership in view, that he began his book as he did.

First of all, in the words of the preface, the author sets forth his purpose in writing, and states his credentials for doing so. These statements constitute a carefully balanced sentence, from the first sonorous word "forasmuch" (ἐπει-δήπερ) to the emphatic "certainty" (ἀσφάλειαν) with which it closes. These statements are indications of the literary and traditional milieu in which Luke was writing, the scope of his work, his claim to be of use, and his view about what his readers needed. The present book sets out to be a somewhat extended commentary on the implications of this one long sentence.

The two halves of this carefully constructed sentence balance each other. Since "many have taken in hand" to write what they knew of the life and teaching of the Lord, so—says Luke—it seemed good to him to do the same, since he could claim to have himself "traced the course of all things accurately from the first."[1] As the contents of earlier writings had been "a narrative of the matters which have been fulfilled among us," so he in turn would "write in order," with a definite plan. As the earlier writings had dealt with the tradition delivered to Christians, so he would also write of the things on which Theophilus had received instruction. And as the evidence for the earlier records was the authority of eyewitnesses and ministers of the word, he would write to give assurance of the truth of what Theophilus and those he represented had already learned.

The balanced form of the preface has a more than literary interest: it implies that Luke is to undertake the same task as his predecessors and to do so as satisfactorily, and, indeed, with his own purpose and readership in view, more satisfactorily. He has been to the trouble to trace all things accurately, or to "follow all things closely" (RSV) and in dealing with the matters "fulfilled among us" will take care to do so "in order." In doing so, his Gospel will deal with events which had a Palestinian setting, and this will be reflected in its language; it will deal with the fulfillment of the Scriptures of the Old Testament, and Luke will make use of the style of the Old Greek (Septuagint) translation; but the preface puts the book into the wider context of the Church in the Roman Empire.

> The literary versatility of the Evangelist is shown at the outset. The Preface is a carefully balanced sentence written in irreproachable literary Greek. After the Preface there is an abrupt change. . . . The transition proves the author to be a conscious artist. He could, if he wished, have written throughout as a professional man of letters; if he does not maintain his polished and polite styles, it is because he judged it unsuitable to transpose the traditional material into another idiom.[2]

---

[1] RSV has "closely" for "accurately," with the latter word as an alternative in the margin, but this makes little difference to Luke's claim. In Acts 18:25, RSV translates the same word as "accurately." It has also "for some time past" instead of "from the first," but in *The Gospel according to St Luke* (London, 1930) J. M. Creed observes that ἄνωθεν is "not to be sharply distinguished from ἀπ' ἀρχῆς." Cf. Acts 26:4, 5.

[2] J. M. Creed, *The Gospel according to St. Luke: The Greek Text, with Introduction, Notes, and Indices* (London: Macmillan, 1930) lxxvi.

We may compare the form of this prefatory sentence with one in Acts (15:24-26): "Forasmuch (ἐπειδή) as we have heard that certain who went out from us have troubled you with words, subverting your souls; to whom we gave no commandment; it seemed good unto us (ἔδοξεν ἡμῖν), having come to one accord, to choose out men and send them unto you with our beloved Barnabas and Paul, men that have hazarded their lives for the name of our Lord Jesus Christ." There is the same balance: "Forasmuch as we have heard . . . it seemed good unto us"; certain men went out to cause trouble, others are being chosen and sent to put things right; the troublemakers went out with no authority, the new emissaries will have authority and include two whose very lives have been the guarantee of their loyalty.

A further connection may be seen with Acts 18:24-25 (where the word καθεξῆς "in order" has just appeared in 18:23) dealing with Apollos: "He was mighty in the scriptures. This man had been instructed in the way of the Lord . . . and taught carefully (ἀκριβῶς, as in Luke 1:3, "accurately" in ASV) the things concerning Jesus, knowing only the baptism of John." The word "instructed" (κατηχήθης) sometimes means no more than "informed" but it appears both in Luke's preface and in Acts 18:25, and for that matter in Acts 21:21, 24, Rom 2:18, 1 Cor 14:19, and Gal 6:6 , to refer to formal instruction.[3] As regards the use of the word "instructed" in the preface, this interpretation is reinforced by the whole tenor of the Gospel and Acts, which are addressed to Christians rather than to others. They represent "the pastoral rather than the missionary element in Christian teaching."[4]

Many, Luke says, had taken in hand to draw up a narrative of the kind he was now writing. Logically this statement could be taken to mean either that a number of such narratives had been produced or, as Farmer has suggested,[5] that many hands had been concerned in the production of *one* narrative. The former has been the more common view, and it has generally been assumed for many years that Luke used one extant document, Mark's Gospel, and at least one other written source (the conjectural 'Q'). Without arguing the case at this point, I need only indicate that the examination of the contents, the method, and the order of

---

[3]Cf. Henry J. Cadbury, "Four Features of Lucan Style," in *Studies in Luke-Acts: Essays Presented in Honor of Paul Schubert*, ed. Leander E. Keck and J. Louis Martyn (Nashville: Abingdon, 1966; repr. Philadelphia: Fortress, 1980) 97. Cadbury's own verdict in his "Commentary on the Preface of Luke" in *The Beginnings of Christianity*, ed. F. J. Foakes Jackson and Kirsopp Lake (London: Macmillan, 1922) 509, is that "probably a neutral translation—'heard'—is safest" in Luke 1:4.

[4]H. J. Cadbury, *The Making of Luke-Acts* (London/New York: Macmillan, 1927) 28.

[5]William R. Farmer, *The Synoptic Problem: A Critical Analysis* (New York/London: Macmillan, 1964; corr. repr. Dillsboro NC: Western North Carolina Press, 1976; dist. Mercer University Press) 222.

Luke's Gospel that is made in the later chapters of this book does, I believe, amply justify Farmer's thesis that the only written source that we know used by Luke (whatever other narratives he may himself have known) was Matthew's Gospel, Mark's being written after both Matthew and Luke. That more than one hand has been concerned in the production of Matthew's Gospel—as I believe—is a possibility which must be taken into account.[6]

But clearly Luke was not only dependent on one written gospel. He wrote from within the Christian Church, with its constant exposition of the tradition of the words and deeds of Christ, and "we have to understand that tradition, in those days, was as formal as it is now informal."[7] It is surprising, wrote Gardner Smith, "that until recently critics have been accustomed to give so little attention to the influence of oral tradition. It seems to have been tacitly assumed that the evangelists wrote in a kind of vacuum in which the Church had been content to live for half a century."[8] The writing of the Gospel must have been influenced by the tradition as Luke had learned it in the meetings of the Church, a tradition carefully memorized and repeated, whether of individual events or teachings, or of more connected narratives such as that of the Passion. Luke was not under the necessity of collecting stray stories embroidered by the fancies of individuals.[9]

It is also clear that even if Luke had Matthew's Gospel before him, there were times when he had a different source (whether oral or written) covering the same material. So there are passages where Luke follows Matthew's text very closely, and other passages that cover substantially the same ground but in which he is either independent of Matthew's text or greatly modifies it. On such occasions it can be either Matthew's or Luke's text that shows the more primitive features.

In three lengthy passages of his Gospel (the Infancy narratives, the Passion stories, and that of the Resurrection appearances) Luke shows an independence from Matthew, although there are features in these passages which correspond to others in Matthew's narrative. There are other points that go back to a tradition common to Luke and John's Gospel, although these probably were independent of each other.

Luke claims what he was writing was in conformity with the tradition of those who were "from the beginning" "eyewitnesses and ministers of the word." "From the beginning" is important. In the record in Acts of the appointment of Matthias, we find that a condition of admission to the number of the Twelve was that of having been among the Christian disciples "all the time that the Lord Jesus went in and out among us, *beginning from the baptism of John*, unto the

---

[6]See the preface, above, vii.

[7]R. O. P. Taylor, *The Groundwork of the Gospels, with Some Collected Papers* (Oxford: Basil Blackwell, 1946) 63.

[8]P. Gardner-Smith, *St John and the Synoptic Gospels* (Cambridge, 1938) 31.

[9]Cf. R. O. P. Taylor, *Groundwork*, 63.

day that he was received up from us" (Acts 1:21-22). In the first chapter of John we have the only explicit record in the Gospels that the experience some at least of the Twelve had of the life of Jesus began from the period of his Baptism. The same Gospel subsequently implies that the Twelve were together from this period, since in John 15:27 Jesus says to the eleven, "Ye also bear witness, because ye have been with me *from the beginning.*" We may also compare John 16:4: "And these things I said not unto you *from the beginning,* because I was with you." For Mark also "the beginning of the gospel of Jesus Christ" (1:1) is at the same point. According to Matthew, it was "from that time" that "Jesus *began* to preach" (4:17), just as in Acts in the speech of Peter in the house of Cornelius he proclaimed the good news "published throughout all Judea, *beginning from Galilee, after the baptism* which John preached" (10:37). So in Luke's Gospel, "Jesus himself, *when he began,* was about thirty years of age" (3:23). (After "began," the ERV adds "to teach" in italics; the RSV adds "his ministry"; the NEB, REB, and NRSV all add "his work.") The intended sense of Acts 1:1-2 ("all that Jesus began both to do and to teach, until the day in which he was received up") is surely not what is often assumed—all that Jesus began in his ministry and now continues in his Church—however true that may be of Christ's work; but "all that Jesus began to do and to teach" and continued to do and to teach until the day he was received up. The "beginning" and the being "received up" are, as will appear again, focal points in the story of Jesus as Luke conceives it; and "the doing and the teaching" are dealt with in turn between them.

Those who were with Jesus from the beginning were the Twelve Apostles, together with an unknown number of other disciples, such as Joseph Barsabbas (Acts 1:23), associated with them. It is to such witness that Luke appeals. He does indeed prefix to the account which begins with the Baptism the narratives of the Infancy for which other evidence than the eyewitness of the Apostles was necessary, but the two chapters dealing with the Infancy are clearly meant to be part of the introduction to the rest of the Gospel of which they are in many ways explanatory, and they illustrate the theme of the Davidic origin of Jesus, itself part of the kerygma of the Apostles.

The form of Luke's words in 1:2, with one definite article controlling both the words "eyewitnesses" and "ministers" implies that the same persons are meant by each.[10] Those who had been eyewitnesses became also ministers of the word (οἱ ἀπ᾽ ἀρχῆς αὐτόπται καὶ ὑπηρέται γενόμενοι τοῦ λόγου). Luke uses the concrete noun "minister" (ὑπηρέτης) as cognate with the abstract noun "service" (διακονία). Paul freely uses the word διάκονος for a minister (e.g., 1 Cor 3:5; 4:1; 2 Cor 3:6; 6:4; 11:15; 12:23) and the corresponding verb διακονέω (e.g., Rom 15:25; 2 Cor 3:3; Philemon 13). In his Gospel, Luke uses the word

---

[10]On Luke 1:2, see A. Feuillet, "Témoins oculaires et serviteurs de la parole," *Novum Testamentum* 15/4 (Leiden, 1973).

διακονέω of ordinary services such as that of Peter's wife's mother (4:39) or Martha (10:40) or of the ministering women (8:3). The word ὑπηρετέω ("to serve/minister to") does not occur in the Gospel, but it is used in Acts ("these hands ministered unto my necessities" 20-34; "friends to minister unto him" 24:23), also of ordinary service.

For Luke the abstract noun διακνοία is a regular word for the work of the apostolate. In Acts 1:17 Judas is said by Peter to have "received his portion in this διακονία" of the apostles. To replace him, lots were cast to choose one "to take his place in this διακονία and apostleship" (1:25). When murmuring arose at the neglect of the Hellenist widows, the Twelve asked for the appointment of seven men of good report so that they themselves might continue "in the διακονία of the word" (6:4), instead of their having to serve (διακονεῖν) tables—the verb again being used of ordinary service. In Acts 12:25 Barnabas and Saul are said to have returned "when they had fulfilled their διακονία; and in 20:24 Paul uses the words "so that I may accomplish my course, and the διακονία which I received from the Lord Jesus, to testify the gospel of the grace of God." The same apostle on coming to Jerusalem "rehearsed one by one the things God had wrought among the Gentiles by his διακονία (21:19).

The corresponding word διάκονος seems to be avoided by Luke perhaps because it had already acquired the specialized sense of "deacon." Whereas in 2 Tim 4:11 there is a reference to the διακονία of Mark, in Acts 13:5 he is referred to not as διάκονος but as ὑπηρέτης.[11] In Acts 26:16 Paul himself is referred to as ὑπηρέτη καὶ μάρτυρα, "a minister and a witness."

To understand the use of ὑπηρέται in Luke 1:2, then, we need to remember not only his use of this word elsewhere but also that of the abstract διακονία. This is regularly used by Luke of the work of the apostles, whether that of the Twelve, of Paul who claimed an equally valid and directly received apostolate with the Twelve, or in one case of Paul and Barnabas together. For Luke, the apostle's mission and the ministry of the word are interchangeable ideas; διακονία is the abstract word he uses for this ministry; for the apostle, the minister, the concrete word is ὑπηρέτης.

If Luke's grammar were pressed and the words of Luke 1:2 read to mean "eyewitnesses of the word" as well as "ministers of the word," it would follow that Luke understood "the word" to include the events of the life of Jesus as well as their proclamation, and was at least approaching the language of 1 John 1:1: "that which we beheld, and our hands handled, concerning the Word of life." But it is unlikely Luke intended this. Creed is right to comment "τοῦ λόγου goes

---

[11]On the use of the word ὑπηρέτης and on the ministry of Mark, see Taylor, *Ground-work of the Gospels*. But if the word has a specific meaning, it is also clear that Luke uses it more widely.

closely with ὑπηρέται."[12] The eyewitnesses of the events became the ministers of the word.

In Lucan usage "the word" means the Gospel in the sense of the Good News proclaimed. In the Third Gospel Luke never uses the word "gospel" at all; and in the Acts only in 15:7 (on the lips of Peter) in the phrase "the word of the gospel," and in 20:24 (on the lips of Paul) in the phrase "the gospel of the grace of God." Behind the New Testament use of the noun is the Old Testament use of the corresponding verb, as a result of which there is some ambivalence, with it being used either of the content of the Good News or of its proclamation. When Paul speaks of "the gospel of the Circumcision" he is using the word in the latter sense—the *preaching* to those of the Circumcision; he may be doing so when he speaks of "my gospel" or "our gospel"; and he frequently uses some qualifying addition: "the gospel of Christ," or "of the glory of Christ," or "of peace," or "of salvation," or "of God."

In a similar way Matthew three times has "the gospel of the kingdom" and only once "this gospel." Mark however has no hesitation about the absolute use of the word. For the one time Mark has "the gospel of Jesus Christ" (1:1) and the one time he has "the gospel of God" (1:14)—both of which are in his introductory verses—there are six times when he uses "the gospel" without qualification. It is a point to which we shall have occasion to return. Luke is more conservative so far as the noun is concerned. He uses the verb from which the noun has taken on its Christian meaning quite freely both in the Gospel and in the Acts (e.g., Luke 1:19; 2:10; 3:18; 4:18; 7:22; Acts 5:42; 8:3; 8:12), with nuances from the sense of "bringing good news" to that of "proclaiming the Gospel."

Luke then does not say "ministers of the Gospel" in his preface but this is strictly the meaning of what he does say. The Gospel is the word of God through and about Jesus, and the task of those whom Christ called was to bear witness to that word.

The first ministers of the word were "eyewitnesses from the beginning." In ordinary usage, "witness" naturally has a double meaning: a man is a witness *of* events when he sees them happen; he is a witness *to* them when he testifies regarding what he has seen. To Luke the duty of bearing testimony arises directly out of the knowledge of the Gospel: in a passage such as Acts 10:39 ("We are witnesses of all things which he did") the idea of testimony is still to the forefront, but the underlying idea of its depending on experience is near the surface. In the preface., however, the important point is the accuracy of the witness and Luke uses the word "eyewitnesses" (αὐτόπται) to make this clear. The narratives of which he speaks, which had dealt with the things fulfilled in

---

[12]Creed, *The Gospel according to St Luke*; see also Feuillet, "Témoins oculaires et serviteurs."

Jesus, were indeed to be shown as in accordance with the testimony (μαρτυρία) of the Apostles; but what also needed affirming was that they were in accordance with the experience of eyewitnesses.

In compiling his Gospel, Luke would no doubt have valued the record of any who had known Jesus, but the real test, which would have to be applied in any case of doubt, would be that of conformity with the tradition of the Apostles themselves. To be steadfast in adherence to apostolic teaching was one of the signs of Church membership (Acts 2:42). Without questioning the loyalty to that teaching in the "many" who had previously compiled a narrative of the things fulfilled in Jesus' life, Luke is asserting his own loyalty to it.

Of the two ideas connected with the word "witness" the first is specified in Luke 1:2 by the word "eyewitnesses," the second by the word "ministers." When Luke wrote, the function of eyewitness was complete, having ended at the Ascension; the testifying to what had been seen, however, continued on. Luke is not likely to have defined in his own mind the moment at which the one function passed into the other. There was in any case a process of appointment, from the first call of disciples until the outpouring of the Holy Spirit at Pentecost. At the end of the Gospel, after the words of our Lord "Ye are witnesses (μάρτυρες) of these things," there comes the promise of the Spirit with the command to tarry in the city, until they are "clothed with power from on high" (Luke 24:48-49). In Acts 5:32 the witness of the Apostles is associated with that of the Spirit, as it is in John 15:26-27. The two functions of witness correspond closely enough with those of the Apostles in the Gospel and in the Acts respectively.

The matters on which Luke was to write were those "fulfilled among us." That by so describing them Luke means more than "accomplished among us" appears from the whole intention of the preface, which was to indicate what the whole book was about. Fulfillment, as we shall see, was one of its leading ideas, a fulfillment in the first place of what, in the Old Testament, God had shown by "all his holy prophets which have been since the world began" (Luke 1:70; Acts 3:21), but ultimately the fulfillment of God's eternal purpose, "the determinate counsel and foreknowledge of God" (Acts 2:23). It has often been remarked how frequently Luke uses the word "must" (δεῖ) both in the Gospel and in the Acts, where it occurs more frequently than in any other book of the New Testament. Not all these uses refer to the idea of fulfillment, but many of them do (e.g. 4:43; 9:22; 17:25), and their very frequency is a reminder of the inevitability Luke saw in the mission of Jesus in fulfillment of the divine purpose. It is the natural conclusion to see this foreshadowed in the language of the preface. Indeed the fact that Jesus fulfilled the promises of God was part of the reassurance that Luke's readers needed to be confident of the certainty concerning the things wherein they had been instructed (1:4).

On these matters Luke asserts that he writes "in order." What Luke means by "order" has also to be judged through the study of the Gospel. It does not necessarily mean a chronological order, though any book which relates the birth, ministry, death, and resurrection of Jesus must conform very broadly to such an order. But it is not necessary that every illustration of the activity of Jesus or of his teaching should follow a chronological scheme, and Luke does not attempt one. He is indeed often careful to avoid giving the impression that he is conforming to or aware of the actual chronological order of the incidents he relates.[13] As we shall see, both the Gospel and the Acts are carefully constructed in a logical order, based on the subject matter dealt with, and indicated by the words of the author himself (Acts 1:1-8). Through this order there also runs a thematic one, concerned with the acceptance or rejection of Christ, which develops from its first beginnings in the infancy narratives of the Gospel to its culmination in the last chapter of Acts. To follow the working out of the order of the Gospel is incidentally the acid test as to whether Luke used Matthew or Mark for much of his material.

Both Luke's Gospel and Acts are dedicated to "Theophilus," and there is no reason to doubt the name refers to a real person. It is most improbable that Luke, who does not write anonymously, would be using the name, by a literary fiction, for the Christian (or other) readers whoever it might happen to be. Nor would the title "most excellent" be a natural form of address in such a case. That in three instances Luke himself records its use for high officials (Acts 23:26; 24:3; 26:25) would suggest that Theophilus was of some official standing. The conventional use of honorific phrases in dedications of books makes this less certain, but even if it is not so the phrase would at least imply that "Theophilus was of a good social position."[14] Theophilus was presumably also a Christian, for while books are dedicated to individuals, they are intended for a wider readership, and the Gospel is addressed to Christians for whom Theophilus stands as a representative. Zahn, indeed, has written:

> The address κράτιστε θεόφιλε not only shows that Theophilus was a man of high position, but also proves that, at the time, he was not a member of the Christian Church; since there is no instance in the Christian literature of the first two centuries where a Christian uses a secular title in addressing another Christian, to say nothing of a title of this character, which may be said to correspond in a general way to "Your Excellency."[15]

---

[13]E.g., see below, 46, 47, 51, 52.

[14]Creed, *The Gospel according to St Luke,* in loc.

[15]Theodor Zahn, *Introduction to the New Testament,* 3 vols., trans. from 3rd German ed. by J. M. Trout, W. A. Mather, et al. (Edinburgh: T.&T. Clark; New York: Scribner's, 1909) 3:44. But Luke's references to "the Lord" in narrative in the Gospel imply he expected his readers—of whom Theophilus was a representative—so to think of Jesus. In the preface, Luke's reference to "the word" without explanation, and to the reliability (ἀσφάλεια) of the information that Theophilus had received, point in the same direction.

On the other hand, there is no reason Luke should not have used a form of address for his own purposes, even if no one also did the same thing. The preface puts Luke's work into the culture of the Roman Empire, and the form of address contributes to this effect. The major fact is surely that the Gospel was written for the reassurance of Christians who had been taught the basic facts of their faith, "the things wherein they were instructed," and that this is the background that Luke ascribes to Theophilus himself. Whoever Theophilus was, it was for Christians in the empire that Luke was writing.

The word "us" in the phrases "fulfilled among us" and "delivered unto us" must refer to the Christian community. In that community the readers are assumed to have some knowledge of the religion of Israel, as is shown, for example, in the first words that follow the preface, which speak of Elizabeth as "of the daughters of Aaron" without explaining the phrase, and of Zacharias entering the temple of the Lord, without explicit mention of Jerusalem. Familiarity with synagogue procedure is assumed in 4:16ff.; so also is some knowledge of Christian faith and practice taken for granted. Some at least of five words of the preface (*fulfilled, delivered, ministers, word, instructed*) which came in time to have a technical ecclesiastical meaning, must already have begun to acquire some of that meaning. In particular, "ministers of the word" is sufficiently technical for it to imply that the reader has some acquaintance with Christian phraseology. Luke is writing for the Church, amplifying and underpinning the instruction its converts had received, by the most reliable, and within the limits of his particular purpose the most complete picture of "all that Jesus began both to do and to teach" (Acts 1:1) that he can paint. This conclusion supports the interpretation of the word "instructed" (κατηχήθης) as meaning definite Christian instruction, which is itself supported by the inherent probability that the word would be so understood by its readers.

The preface tells us why Luke felt it incumbent on him to write. In doing so, it raises many questions. If many had taken in hand to draw up a narrative already, what can we know of the sources available to Luke? What was the tradition to which he felt bound to conform? What were his methods in writing? If he wrote "in order," what kind of order can we discern in his book? What did he understand by things being *fulfilled*? What can we know of him as a person, or of the readers represented by Theophilus? It is to such questions that the following chapters are addressed.

Chapter 2

The Sources of the Gospel

Forasmuch as many have taken in hand to draw up a narrative. . . . –Luke 1:1

The State of the Question

Luke himself makes it clear that he was not the first to compile a narrative of "those matters which have been fulfilled among us," and the close correspondence, not only of subject matter but also in words and order, between large parts of Luke's Gospel with those of Matthew and Mark raises the question of the relationships between them.

It has for a long time been almost the orthodoxy of criticism that Matthew and Luke have used two main sources, Mark and Q, the latter a hypothetical document or collection of materials, largely consisting of the discourses of our Lord. How much this is taken for granted can be seen, for example, in the first sentence following the preface of Dennis E. Nineham's commentary on Mark: "As most readers will know, when St Matthew and St Luke were writing they both had copies of Mark in front of them and incorporated almost the whole of it into their Gospels."[1] The commentator is rather less dogmatic with regard to Q: "St Matthew and St Luke also appear to have used another common source, in addition to Mark, which is usually known as 'Q'."[2]

Behind a confidence such as that of Nineham about what "most readers will know" lies a long history. For long centuries the opinion of Augustine that Mark was an abbreviation of Matthew had not been seriously challenged. The relation of Luke to either Matthew or Mark had received less attention. The first significant break came in a book by an almost forgotten author. In 1764, Henry Owen, the rector of St. Olave's Church in the City of London, published his *Observations on the Four Gospels* in which, with a modification of the Augustinian hypothesis, he sought to show that Mark had been dependent on both

---

[1]Dennis E. Nineham, *The Gospel of St. Mark* (Baltimore: Penguin Books, 1963; New York: Seabury Press, 1968; Philadelphia: Westminster Press, 1978) 11.

[2]Ibid.

Matthew and Luke. The chronological order of the Gospels was therefore
Matthew, Luke, and Mark. Owen's book might have had little influence had not
the great German textual critic Johann J. Griesbach been in London during
1769–1770 and—as the researches of Bernard Orchard have shown—acquired
Owen's book. Griesbach produced the first modern synopsis of the first three
Gospels, and incidentally added the phrase "Synoptic Gospels" to our language.
In 1783, and more fully in his *Commentatio* in 1779–1780,[3] Griesbach developed,
much on the same lines as Owen, the claim that Mark was dependent on
Matthew and Luke, and that Mark often alternated in his primary use of one or
other of them, with Matthew as the source most frequently used though with
Luke still in mind. As with earlier writers, the main interest in Griesbach's
Commentatio was in the relationship of Mark to Matthew and Luke, with less
concern about that of Luke with Matthew.

So the "Griesbach hypothesis" came to the notice of the scholarly world, but
it already had a rival which later was to supplant it for many years. Already
G. C. Storr of Tübingen had put forward a revolutionary hypothesis: that Mark
was prior to Matthew and Luke, and used by both of them. Griesbach himself
was at some pains to refute Storr's arguments, but the theory that Storr had put
forward was to have an increasing influence in later years. For the next half
century, however, Griesbach's view was widely held.

The great change came in the latter half of the nineteenth century. The
publication of H. J. Holtzmann's book on the Synoptic Gospels in 1863 and his
subsequent writings began an era in which critical opinion in Germany swung
right round to the acceptance of Marcan priority, and this has been the commonly
accepted view of German scholarship down to this day. While Roman Catholic
scholars like Lagrange, with a greater confidence in the value of early tradition,
still defended the priority of Matthew, they understood this as meaning the
priority of an original Aramaic Matthew, the canonical text of the Greek
Matthew being partly dependent on Mark. What they taught was therefore in
effect a compromise with the hypothesis of Marcan priority. Their work, like that
of John Chapman and B. C. Butler when these came to challenge the whole
hypothesis, was for long largely discounted as being conditioned by the necessity
of conforming to an official ecclesiastical line.

The influence of German scholarship on that of England was very great. The
resultant situation may be illustrated by the first sentence of William Sanday in
the compilation he edited, *Studies in the Synoptic Problem*: "We assume what is
commonly known as the 'Two-Document Hypothesis' ";[4] or by the description

---

[3]The *Commentatio* is reprinted in the original Latin and with an English translation
in *J. J. Griesbach: Synoptic and Text-Critical Studies, 1776–1976,* ed. Bernard Orchard
and Thomas R. W. Longstaff (Cambridge/New York: Cambridge University Press, 1978)
74-135.

[4](Oxford: Clarendon Press, 1911).

of this hypothesis by J. C. Hawkins (one of the contributors to the Sanday volume) in his *Horae synopticae* as "a practically certain result of modern study of the 'Synoptic Problem'."[5] This was the outlook that reached its classical expression in B. H. Streeter's *The Four Gospels*.[6] It is from this point that we need to consider the later developments and the slow erosion of confidence in the hypothesis of Marcan priority in England, and—especially because of the work of William R. Farmer—in America.

Streeter's case may be summarized as follows: "Matthew may be regarded as an enlarged edition of Mark"; Luke, with a different plan, incorporates large sections of Mark. Matthew has most of Mark's materials, and Luke more than half of it, in language that is "very largely identical" with Mark's words. When the three Gospels have the same episode to deal with, Mark's words, if not found in both, are to be found in one or the other. As regards order, both Matthew and Luke usually correspond to that of Mark, and when this is not true of one of them, it is usually true of the other. From these facts the conclusion is drawn that they must be incorporating into their Gospels "a source identical, or all but identical, with Mark."[7]

In support of this basic case, Streeter claims that the primitive character of Mark is revealed also by his inclusion of phrases that might cause offense to his readers, and by the presence of Aramaic words which they would not understand (though he regularly translates them), both of these characteristics being omitted by Matthew and Luke. Further, Streeter claims the style and grammar of Mark are rougher than those of Matthew and Luke who set out to improve on Mark.

To this Marcan hypothesis Streeter, in common of course with many others, adds that the existence of much other common material in Matthew and Luke, which is not derived from Mark, presupposes a further document ('Q'), now no longer extant. There are some episodes or sayings, such as the Beelzebul controversy or the parable of the Mustard Seed, which occur in both Mark and Q, and the question also sometimes arises whether Mark himself knew Q.

There are points of agreement between Matthew and Luke which remain unexplained on this hypothesis. Streeter accounts for them in different ways: there may have been a version in Q parallel to that of Mark; or the attempt by Matthew and Luke to improve Mark's style may have resulted in their making the same corrections; or the manuscripts in which the Gospels have been preserved may have been corrupted by a scribe assimilating one text to another. Streeter thinks that this last was the most common cause.

---

[5]Subtitle: *Contributions to the Study of the Synoptic Problem* (Oxford: Clarendon Press, 1909; [1]1899) 115.

[6]Subtitle: *A Study of Origins, Treating of the Manuscript Tradition, Sources, Authorship, and Dates* (London: Macmillan, 1924ff.; New York: St. Martin's Press, 1956ff.).

[7]Streeter, *The Four Gospels*, 181.

For good measure, Streeter adds one further major hypothesis that Luke, or perhaps someone before the author of the present Third Gospel, combined material special to Luke (for which Streeter has the symbol 'L') with Q to form a document that might be called Proto-Luke; the present Third Gospel is a combination of Proto-Luke with Mark.

For our purpose here, we shall not need to discuss the Proto-Luke hypothesis further. It is part of our argument here that the whole Marcan hypothesis (that Mark is the basis of much of the First and Third Gospels) is mistaken, and that carries with it the rejection of the Q-hypothesis also and the Proto-Luke theory which depends on that. "It is important to recognize that these two hypotheses (Q and Proto-Luke) hang together; take away the Q hypothesis and the Proto-Luke hypothesis cannot stand."[8] As it is part of the present study to show that the Q hypothesis is unnecessary, we need not concern ourselves further here with Proto-Luke as Streeter imagined it. The same title Proto-Luke has however been more recently used with a somewhat different understanding by M.-É. Boismard, and we shall meet it again in discussing his own contribution to Synoptic studies.[9]

The basic facts cited by Streeter are not in dispute, but it in no way follows that he draws the right conclusions from them. A curious blindness to other possibilities seems sometimes to have afflicted critics who have taken the priority of Mark as the most assured result of New Testament criticism. Contradictory conclusions may often be drawn from the same evidence. As a typical example, I take the story in Mark 12:41-44 and Luke 21:1-4 of the Widow's Offering in the temple. Mark tells the story in seventy-five words, Luke in fifty-eight. Mark says Jesus "sat down over against the treasury, and beheld how the multitude cast money into the treasury"; Luke says Jesus "looked up, and saw the rich men that were casting their gifts into the treasury." Luke says the widow gave two *lepta*; Mark adds "that is, a *quadrans*." Mark says she cast her money "into the treasury"; Luke says "into the gifts." Mark makes Jesus say "Amen" where Luke makes him say "Truly."

Now alternative explanations are possible. Luke may have abbreviated Mark's wordiness or Mark may have retold Luke's story in a more verbose way. Either Mark's "sat down" or Luke's "looked up" may be from an independent reminiscence, or Mark may have added "sat down" because earlier (11:27) he had Jesus "walking in the temple." Mark may have added "that is, a *quadrans*" in explanation of Luke's two *lepta*, or Luke (though less naturally) may have omitted to translate into the terms of Roman coinage. Mark may have simply repeated the word "treasury" (strictly a room, to which the widow would not

---

[8]C. K. Barrett, *Luke the Historian in Recent Study* (London: Epworth, 1961) 20.

[9]In, e.g., Pierre Benoit and M.-É. Boismard, *Synopse des quatre Evangiles en français, avec parallèles des apocryphes et des Pères*, 3 vols. (Paris: Editions du Cerf, 1965–1977; 2nd ed. rev. and corr. by P. Sandevoir, 2 vols., 1972).

have access) where Luke uses "gifts," accurately referring to the kind of chest (*corbana*, cf. Matt 27:6) into which money for the treasury was actually put.[10] Luke may have translated Mark's "Amen" to "Truly," or Mark may have retranslated to an obvious original. Luke may have been attracted by Mark's story of a widow, but his own more obvious interest in widows would account for the inclusion of the story independently. At least it can be seen that Marcan priority cannot be assumed on evidence such as the story provides. Indeed, without the acceptance of that priority on other grounds, the more natural interpretation, in view of Luke's own special interests, is that Mark's story is derived from Luke.

Matthew also has his special interests, among them the inclusion of Old Testament quotations. A similar case, this time concerned with the relation of Matthew and Mark, is therefore to be found in the pericope of the Reason for Parables (Matt 13:10-15; Mark 4:10-12; Luke 8:9-10). Behind the words of all three Synoptists lies a reference to Isa 6:9-10, which is also quoted in Acts 28:26-27 and partially in John 12:40. It may well have been one of a stock of testimonia used by the early Christians. Matthew's record of Jesus' own words closes with the phrase "they did not understand" (συνιοῦσιν). Matthew then adds one of his formal quotations, introduced by saying "with them is fulfilled the prophecy of Isaiah," and Isa 6:9-10 is quoted in full. Luke does not include this. What is significant is that Mark does add μήποτε ἐπιστρέψωσιν καὶ ἀφεθῇ αὐτοῖς, an abridged form of the latter part of Matthew's quotation "lest (μήποτε) they should perceive with their eyes, and hear with their ears, and understand (συνῶσεν) and turn again and I should heal them (ἐπιστρέψωσιν καὶ ἰάσομαι αὐτους)."

There are two conceivable alternatives: first, that if Matthew was using Mark's text, he saw the Isaianic reference and went back to its source for the full quotation. And in that case, when Luke used Mark, he stopped short of Mark's last five words, presumably for the sake of brevity. Alternatively, if Mark used Matthew, whose use of the formal quotation is characteristic, he merely abridged Matthew's words, not quite accurately, skipping from the word συνιοῦσιν of Matt 13:13 to the συνῶσεν of 13:15. Luke's own text does not then call for explanation: he simply stopped short of the formal quotation. Either alternative is possible, but Matthew's usage with regard to Old Testament quotations makes the second the more plausible.

There are many other instances where the evidence can be interpreted in contrary ways, at least when each is looked at in isolation. Mark, for example, has a special fondness for double phrases, seen both when he is parallel with Matthew and Luke, and at other times. When he is in parallel, the question arises whether the Marcan text is the original or a conflation of Matthew and Luke. So,

---

[10]Cf. Benoit and Boismard, *Synopse*, in loc.

when at 1:32 Mark has "at even, when the sun did set," either interpretation seems equally possible. To judge between them it is necessary to look at a wider range of examples. Sir John Hawkins set out a list of such duplicate expressions in his *Horae synopticae*, and commented that

> It used to be thought that in such passages . . . Mark had put together phrases from Matthew and Luke. But after looking through all these instances of Mark's habitual manner of duplicate expression, it will appear far more probable that . . . in these cases Matthew happened to adopt one of them and Luke the other, whereas in some other cases, e.g. Mk 2:25; 14:43 . . . they both happened to adopt the same one.[11]

Hawkins surely did not look closely enough. The following is a list of the clearest examples (not all noticed by Hawkins) where the three texts are running parallel and where either Matthew and Luke must have selected from Mark or Mark has conflated Matthew and Luke. For easy comparison, Mark's double phrases may be divided as A and B.

		Mark		**Matthew and Luke**	
1.	1:12-13	A	into the wilderness	Matt 4:1	into the wilderness
		B	and he was in the wilderness	Luke 4:1	in the wilderness
2.	1:32	A	at even	Matt 8:6	when even was come
		B	when the sun did set	Luke 4:40	when the sun was setting
3.	1:32	A	all that were sick	Luke 4:40	any sick with divers diseases
		B	and them that were possessed with demons	Matt 8:16	many possessed with demons
4.	1:42	A	the leprosy departed from him	Luke 5:13	the leprosy departed from him
		B	and he was cleansed	Matt 8:3	his leprosy was cleansed
5.	2:1	A	into Capernaum	Matt 9:1	into his own city
		B	after (some) days	Luke 5:17	on one of those days
6.	2:25	A	when he had need	Matt 12:3	
		B	and was hungry	&Luke 6:3	when he was hungry
7.	4:21	A	under the bushel	Matt 5:15	under the bushel
		B	or under the bed	Luke 8:16	under the bed
8.	5:1,3	A	out of the tombs (μνημείων)	Matt 8:28	out of the tombs (μνημείων)
		B	in the tombs (μνήμασιν)	Luke 8:27	in the tombs (μνήμασιν)
9.	5:12	A	send us into the swine	Matt 8:31	send us away into the herd of swine
		B	that we may enter into them	Luke 8:32	leave to enter into them
10.	5:21	A	he saw a tumult	Matt 9:24	making a tumult
		B	people weeping	Luke 8:52	all were weeping
11.	5:34	A	go in peace	Luke 8:48	go in peace
		B	and be healed of thy plague	Matt 9:22	and the woman was made whole

---

[11]*Horae synopticae. Contributions to the Study of the Synoptic Problem*, 2nd ed. rev. and suppl. (Oxford: Clarendon Press, 1909; [1]1899) 142.

12. 6:16	A John whom I beheaded	Luke 9:9	John I beheaded
	B has been raised	Matt 14:1	he has been raised
13. 8:34	A he called unto him the multitude	Luke 9:23	he said unto all
	B with his disciples	Matt 16:24	then said Jesus unto his disciples
14. 10:29	A for my sake	Matt 19:29	for my name's sake
	B and for the sake of the gospel	Luke 18:29	for the sake of the kingdom of God
15. 10:36	A and they come to Jericho	Luke 18:35	as he drew nigh unto Jericho
	B and as he went out from Jericho	Matt 20:29	and as they went out from Jericho
16. 11:2	A immediately	Matt 21:2	immediately
	B as you enter	Luke 19:10	as you enter
17. 12:14-15	A tribute to Caesar or not	Matt 22:17	tribute to Caesar or not
	B shall we give or not give	&Luke 20:21	
18. 13:1	A what manner of stones	Luke 21:5	adorned with costly stones
	B and what manner of building	Matt 24:1	the building of the temple
19. 14:1	A the passover	Matt 26:2	the passover
	B and the unleavened bread	Luke 22:1	the feast of unleavened bread
20. 14:12	A the first day	Matt 26:17	the first (day)
	B when they sacrificed the passover	Luke 22:7	on which the passover must be sacrificed
21. 14:30	A today	Luke 22:24	this day
	B this night	Matt 26:34	this night
22. 14:40	A immediately	Matt 26:47	
	B while he was still speaking	&Luke 22:47	while he was still speaking
23. 16:1	A with the elders	Matt 27:1	and the elders
	B and scribes	Luke 22:66	and scribes

Since on the Marcan hypothesis both Matthew and Luke could choose between the A and B phrases, and have indeed chosen from both, then on the law of averages one would expect both Matthew and Luke to have chosen A and B half the times each, that is, about eleven or twelve times each. In fact, Matthew has A thirteen times and B ten times, and Luke has A nine times and B fourteen times. This is quite the kind of result one would expect. But on the same law of averages one would expect Matthew and luke to choose the same phrase as each other, whether A or B, half the times also. In fact in only three instances, numbered 6, 17, and 22, do they have the same choice. On the theory of Marcan priority it is a wildly improbable result. The natural conclusion is that the reverse process has taken place: Mark conflating the texts of Matthew and Luke, and in three instances independently following his own common tendency to double phrases (in one of them, number 22, merely adding his frequent "immediately"). If we also add the seven examples (Mark 2:20; 4:5; 4:39; 4:40; 6:36; 13:28; 13:29) in Hawkins's list where either Matthew or Luke has both A and B, we find that in none of these do both agree in using the same double expression. Out of the increased total of thirty examples, it is still only in three instances that Matthew and Luke would have made the same choice. This only reinforces the case for Mark having used Matthew and Luke.

A detailed examination of all the doublets in Mark that have parallels in Matthew and Luke appears in appendix 2 of my *The Making of Mark* ("Duality in Mark," 219-27), with the conclusion that there is strong support for the hypothesis that Mark is dependent on Matthew and Luke, and that "Mark sometimes used a phrase from Matthew or Luke and expanded it, and when they used different phrases he often combined them."[12]

A year after the appearance of Streeter's *The Four Gospels*, a note of warning was sounded in Charles F. Burney's *Poetry of Our Lord*. Burney himself assumed the priority of Mark and the existence of Q, but his careful analysis of the structure of the sayings of our Lord in the Gospels convinced him that Mark, at any rate on occasion, did not show a more primitive character than either Matthew or Luke. "Thirdly," he wrote, "as regards the Marcan source in relation to its parallels in the other Synoptists, we have gleaned a few clear indications that blind confidence in Mark, as necessarily preserving the most original form of sayings that are supposed to be derived from him, is wrong."[13] Burney then gives three cases (Mark 8:35; 18:27; 14:7) on which he concludes that "Mark has glossed the original." The evidence in such cases is one of the matters we must later discuss. Since Burney accepted the Q hypothesis, he could find it necessary to appeal to Q even for a passage common to all three evangelists (Mark 2:19-22; Matt 9:15-17; Luke 5:34-39), with a long footnote including the words "May we not infer from these facts that the passage really belonged originally to Q, and was derived thence by Mark less faithfully than by Matthew?"[14] To a further passage (Mark 8:34-38; Matt 16:24-27; Luke 9:23-26) Burney again appended a footnote, concluding "It would seem to follow that this also is originally a Q passage, which Matthew has preserved more accurately in the main than Mark."[15] What Burney does not seem to envisage is the possibility that Matthew, and not Q, is the source of the Marcan passage.

The significance of Burney's warnings was taken up later by B. C. Butler who, in his *The Originality of St. Matthew*,[16] carried the discussion over a wider area, without however trying to set out a full exposition of the literary history of the Synoptics. As his title suggested, Butler was concerned primarily to show the originality of Matthew over against Mark, and Luke was less in his purview. Within these limits, Butler's work is of permanent value, and it clearly demonstrated that a scholar was not bound to hold that the priority of Mark was proved once and for all. At one particular point, Butler made a good case that Matthew reveals a direct quotation from Aramaic, and one not dependent on the Marcan

---

[12]Harold Riley, *The Making of Mark: An Exploration* (Macon GA: Mercer University Press, 1989) 227.

[13]*The Poetry of Our Lord: An Examination of the Formal Elements of Hebrew Poetry in the Discourses of Jesus Christ* (Oxford: Clarendon Press, 1925) 85.

[14]Ibid., 35.

[15]Ibid., 141-42.

[16]*The Originality of St. Matthew: A Critique of the Two-Document Hypothesis* (Cambridge: Cambridge University Press, 1951).

parallel, at 27:33: "And coming to a place called Golgotha, that is, the place of a skull."

Twenty-five years later, Butler has written of the Two-Document hypothesis (that Matthew and Luke used Mark and Q): "I still hold it to be highly questionable, though I should not today sponsor the alternative hypothesis propounded in *The Originality of Matthew*."[17] The importance of Butler's book does not however depend on the acceptance of his "alternative hypothesis" but on his insistence that while it is true that there is, as almost every scholar would agree, a literary connection between Mark and both Matthew and Luke, it does not inevitably follow that this is due to the latter two having used Mark as a source. Butler opened a door, and it has not since been closed. It has at least been accepted that while Mark is a "middle term" between the other two, other hypotheses would account for this equally well.

In a fresh defense of Marcan priority and in answering Butler, G. M. Styler makes this admission and bases his case on more general grounds.[18] For Styler the strongest argument for Marcan priority is "that based on the freshness and circumstantial character" of Mark's narrative, and he suggests that it was Mark's connection with Peter which accounts for this and renders resort to Matthew unnecessary. On the other hand, there is no reason why, if Mark was using Matthew and Luke as his base, he should not in his more colloquial style have added circumstantial details he had heard in Christian preaching—Mark did not live in a vacuum. It has to be remembered, if Mark heard Peter's teaching, that Papias has stated that Peter "adapted his instructions to the χρείας." Those who quote these words have generally translated χρείας as "needs," and then added in brackets such words as "of the hearers." So translated the statement does not seem to have much point: what teacher does not have the needs of his hearers in mind? But if R. O. P. Taylor is correct in his interpretation of the word,[19] no bracketed explanation is needed, and it means just such short narratives as Mark (or Matthew or Luke) used, and Peter's having used them would adequately account for Mark's details.

For Styler the argument that "puts the priority of Mark beyond serious doubt" is that Matthew sometimes goes astray "yet betrays a knowledge of the authentic version—the version given by Mark";[20] and he gives the account of the death of John Baptizer (Mark 6:17-29; Matt 14:3-12) as an example, but this is very unconvincing. A comparison of the text does indeed make it clear that either

---

[17]*The Clergy Review* (May 1976): 199.

[18]In "The Priority of Mark," excursus 4 in *The Birth of the New Testament*, by C. F. D. Moule, 223-32 (London: A.&C. Black; New York: Harper & Row, 1962; 3rd ed. rev. San Francisco: Harper & Row, 1982: 285-316); 1st ed. cited here.

[19]Taylor, *The Groundwork of the Gospels, with Some Collected Papers* (Oxford: Basil Blackwell, 1946) 75ff.

[20]Styler, "The Priority of Mark," 229.

Matthew used Mark or Mark use Matthew. The statement in Matthew that Herod
wanted John killed, to which Styler takes exception, is historically probable, it
is in line with that of Luke 13:31 about Jesus ("Herod wants to kill you"), and
is merely expanded by Mark to bring in Herodias in view of what follows.
Mark's statement that Herod heard John gladly, itself very similar to Luke 23:8
about Herod and Jesus, is an inference of Mark which cannot be pressed. The
narrative in Matt 14:3-12 follows naturally on Matt 14:1-2, which deals with
Herod's opinion of Jesus as "John the Baptist, raised from the dead." The
narrative in Mark 6:17-29 follows on the longer text of Mark 6:14-16, which is
closer to that of Luke 9:7-9, which with its inclusion as in Luke of references to
Elijah and the prophets, makes a less natural connection with what follows.
Whereas Matthew refers to "John the Baptist" (14:2) Luke merely has "John"
and Mark has added "the Baptizer" (as in 1:4). That is predictable, if Mark is
adding to Luke rather than copying Matthew. When at 6:25 Mark is parallel to
Matthew, he uses the same form as Matthew, "the Baptist," but in his own extra
material at 6:24 he uses the form for "the Baptizer" again. At the close of the
story, Matthew resumes with a natural connection: John's disciples "went and
told Jesus; now when Jesus heard this he withdrew." Luke, who has not used the
story of the Baptist's death, has an equally natural continuation, as he has been
dealing with the mission of the Twelve, with the words "the apostles returned."
Mark, who like Matthew has had the same reference to John's disciples burying
him, surprisingly continues not as in Matthew but as in Luke, with "the apostles
returned." The natural inference is that Mark has turned from Luke to Matthew
at 6:17 and back again from Matthew to Luke at 6:30. The awkwardness of
Mark's transitions both before and after the account of the Baptist's death points
to his dependence on both Matthew and Luke, the story itself being derived from
Matthew and told in a more expanded form.

Styler deals carefully with the issues raised by Butler, but his own answers
are open to question. One further example must here suffice. Styler repeats the
argument that there are what he calls "well-known examples where Mark's
version appears to be lacking in respect for the apostles or even in its estimate
of the person of Christ, and where Matthew's version avoids such implications."[21]
In a footnote Styler refers to the text which perhaps more than any other has
been quoted as showing that Matthew *must* have modified Mark (Matt 19:16-22;
Mark 10:17-22; Luke 18:18-23), and says that Matthew's question "Why do you
ask me about the good?" and his comment εἷς ἐστιν ὁ ἀγαθός are "intelligible
as a rewriting of Mark, but most odd otherwise." It is incredible that Mark, or
Luke who has the same words, should be thought to raise any doubt of Christ's
goodness, and no early writer drew this conclusion from the text. If Matthew in
using Mark had thought so, he would have been a surprising exception. But if,

---

[21]"The Priority of Mark," 228.

as on the Griesbach hypothesis, Luke (who was copied by Mark) used Matthew, he did face a difficulty. What was odd to Styler was already odd to Luke. To what or to whom did εἷς ἐστιν ὁ ἀγαθός, "the good [masc.] is one," refer? The natural inference for one with Luke's background (and now an easy one for anyone familiar with Luke's version) was that the masculine ἀγαθός must mean God, and so the introduction had to be amended to account for this. In his book *Matthew, a Scribe Trained for the Kingdom of Heaven*, O. Lamar Cope has defended Matthew's version as the original, and has argued that "the good" refers not to God but to Torah (νόμος).[22] Whether or not this is sound, the account is a straightforward Jewish-Christian narrative: the question about doing good is answered by pointing to God, or to his good Law, for his will is illustrated in the commandments, and "What good thing shall I do to inherit eternal life?" is clearly answered, as it is not in Luke or Mark, in the words "If you would enter life." The narrative is a very insecure basis for a judgment of Marcan priority.

The challenge that had been thrown down by Butler's book was taken up in 1964 by William R. Farmer in a radical reappraisal of the whole Synoptic Problem in his book of that name.[23] Reviewing the history of Synoptic criticism from Griesbach onwards, Farmer came down firmly in support of Griesbach's own hypothesis. As a corollary, he made his own suggestion as to why when Matthew and Luke were available, Mark should have been written at all, and it has often been objected since that there could be no good reason. But Farmer would agree that his own solution is not the only possible answer, and that the Griesbach hypothesis does not depend on it. Farmer paid less attention to the purpose of Luke, and it is with Luke that the present study is concerned. The study of Luke will, I believe, give added and convincing support to Farmer's case.

Before attempting a summary of the case Farmer has presented we may notice that while his arguments have not been convincing to many other scholars and have not always been given the attention they deserve, a gradual shift was taking place in reliance on Marcan priority even before Farmer published his work in 1964. More recent writers have seemed to be less sure about Q, even though they still accept the priority of Mark. For instance, a recent small commentary on Luke, which assumed that Matthew used Mark, includes the words: "Most scholars believe that, instead of Luke using Matthew, they both used a (now vanished) document called 'Q.' But I have followed the minority who believe that Luke used Matthew."[24] This is the position which was adopted

---

[22]Catholic Biblical Quarterly Monograph Series 5 (Washington DC: Catholic Biblical Association of America, 1976).

[23]*The Synoptic Problem: A Critical Analysis* (New York/London: Macmillan, 1964; corr. repr. Dillsboro NC: Western North Carolina Press, 1976; dist. Mercer University Press).

[24]John Drury, *Luke*, J. B. Phillips Commentaries (London: Fontana Books; New York: Macmillan, 1973).

by Austin M. Farrer, who with characteristic ingenuity could in his *St Matthew and St Mark*[25] deal with the "Matthaean reconstruction of Mark," whom he regarded as the earliest of the evangelists, and in his essay "On Dispensing with Q"[26] came out clearly for the use of Matthew by Luke. In Farrer's view Q becomes unnecessary, for Matthew used Mark and Luke used Mark and Matthew. That certainly covers some but, as we shall see, not all of the evidence. Farrer concluded:

> The Q hypothesis is not, of itself, a probable hypothesis. It is simply the sole alternative to the supposition that St Luke had read St Matthew (or vice versa). It needs no refutation except the demonstration that its alternative is possible. It hangs on a single thread; cut that, and it falls by its own weight.[27]

A very different theory has been put forward in a more recent book, the second volume of the Benoit-Boismard *Synopsis of the Four Gospels in French*, to which reference has already been made. Benoit's preface contains the warning that he is not himself in entire agreement, though he records his admiration for *le travail acharné* of his colleague Boismard, as well he might. Boismard himself describes his theory as *passablement complexe*. Omitting the elements that concern the Fourth Gospel as outside our present purview, the theory, so far as it concerns our present subject, may be summarized as follows:

(1) There were four original sources, which Boismard calls documents A, B, C, and Q. Q may have been in fact not a single document, but for comparative simplicity it is referred to as a unit.

(2) A combination of these sources resulted in the production of an Intermediate-Matthew, Intermediate-Mark, and Proto-Luke.

(3) The canonical Luke is derived from Proto-Luke, Intermediate-Mark, and (through Proto-Luke) Intermediate-Matthew. And it is important to note that the final edition of Mark is said to be marked by many "Lucanisms," often in groups together. "Would Luke," Boismard asks, "be the one who put the final hand to Mark's Gospel? It is possible, but one could think also of a disciple of Luke, strongly impregnated with his vocabulary and style."[28]

It is not part of our present concern to investigate the evidence for the primary sources (A, B, C, and Q) Boismard seeks to identify. What his theory

---

[25]Edward Cadbury Lectures 1953–1954 (Westminster, England: Dacre Press, 1954).

[26]In *Studies in the Gospels: Essays in Memory of R. H. Lightfoot*, ed. Dennis E. Nineham, 55-88 (Oxford: Basil Blackwell, 1955).

[27]Ibid., 62.

[28]Benoit and Boismard, *Synopse des quatre Evangiles en français*, 2:28. That there are "Lucanisms," often in groups, had already been seen by Farmer, as arising from Mark's alternate adherence to Matthew's or Luke's order, and from corresponding closeness to Matthew's or Luke's text. See below.

has in common with other less complicated systems is that Luke has used Mark (or more precisely, in Boismard's view, Intermediate-Mark), and if it can be shown that this is groundless, some at least of his complications disappear.

The Evidence

Before returning to the general question as dealt with by Farmer, it will be convenient to look more closely at Boismard's argument. It is largely based on a painstaking analysis of the use of particular words. To indicate their relative frequency in the New Testament Boismard uses groups of figures (e.g., 3/1/9/0/17) to indicate the number of times a word occurs in Matthew/Mark/Luke/John/Acts, with sometimes a sixth figure for the rest of the New Testament. It will be convenient here to follow this practice.

The Achilles' heel of Boismard's scheme is his insistence that while Luke used Intermediate-Mark, the canonical Mark has been finally revised by Luke, or by a "Lucan," someone influenced by Luke's style. The three following examples are chosen to include one passage where Mark and Luke are in parallel, one where there are connections in the context, and one where there is no parallel to Mark's narrative in Luke.

(1) The Gerasene Demoniac (Mark 5:1-20; Luke 8:26-39). After recording the casting out of demons, Mark 5:15 and Luke 8:35 both say that the man who had been possessed was then "clothed." Only Luke had previously said that he had worn no clothes. Moreover, "Mark and Luke have in common words never read elsewhere in Mark, but which are relatively frequent in Luke, and typical of his style." These are:

Mark 5:7 : "Most High" ὑψίστος : 0/1/5/0/2/1.
Mark 5:14 : "what had happened" τὸ γεγονός : 0/1/5/0/2/0.
Mark 5:16 : "how" (πῶς) after verbs to "announce" or "declare" : cf. Luke 8:36; Acts 9:27; 11:13; 12:17.

To these references Boismard later adds this comment: "At vv. 16 and 19, one finds in Mark the words 'announce' and 'declare,' which are also read in Luke, but not in the same order ("announce" at vv. 34, 36; "declare" at v. 39); these two words are Lucan rather than Marcan (ἀπαγγέλλω : 8/2/11/1/16; διηγέομαι : 0/2/2/0/3/1)."[29]

All these "Lucanisms" are in the parallel passage of Luke. If they had been found in an entirely unrelated passage, they might have had the significance Boismard accords to them. But since Mark and Luke are running in parallel, the most obvious explanation when Lucan words occur in Mark is that Mark is copying Luke and uses words that might not otherwise occur to him. It is impossible to deduce that Luke's Gospel, here at any rate, is dependent on Mark.

---

[29]Benoit and Boismard, Synopse, 2:206. Boismard transliterates the Greek; for the sake of consistency I have restored the Greek letters.

The story of the Gerasene demoniac is part of a series where, on the Griesbach hypothesis it is natural to see that Mark was following Luke's order; it is not therefore surprising that Lucan echoes should be found in it. To quote Farmer, "This is a very clear exmple of the phenomenon of a positive correlation between agreement in order and agreement in wording."[30]

(2) The Great Commandment (Mark 12:32-34). In Mark 12:32-34 we have a section without parallel in either Matthew or Luke; the previous verses (12:28-31) are paralleled by Matt 22:34-40 and Luke 10:25-28. Mark is here however following Matthew's order, and the Lucan parallel to his preceding pericope is Luke 20:27-40. The influence of this section may well be seen in Mark 12:32 καλῶς διδάσκαλε ἐπ' ἀληθείας εἶπες corresponding to Luke 20:39 διδάσκαλε, καλῶς εἶπας and in Mark 12:34 οὐδεὶς οὐκέτι ἐτόλμα αὐτὸν ἐπερωτῆσαι corresponding to Luke 20:40 οὐκέτι γὰρ ἐτόλμων ἐπερωτᾶν αὐτὸν οὐδέν. So far, the evidence is consistent with Mark's having used Luke. Boismard's case, however, is that in v. 31, which is without parallel in Luke, a "Lucan" hand is visible. The examples are as follows:

Mark 12:32 : "except" πλήν : 5/1/15/0/4/6. If followed by the genitive, as here, only in Luke three times.

Mark 12:33 : Mark has "understanding" σύνεσις instead of "soul" as in 12:30 and parallels. σύνεσις occurs in Luke 2:47 and five times in Paul.

Mark 12:34 : "far" μακράν : 1/1/2/1/3/2.

The last of these (μακράν) is hardly significant; nor is the use of πλήν with the genitive; this is not a common Lucan usage, and in fact Mark is quoting Deut 4:35, where this phrase occurs in the Septuagint. As to σύνεσις, this is rather a variant of διανοία, which has just been used in Mark 12:31 (Matt 22:37; Luke 10:27), and Lucan influence would rather have caused that word to be used here. This is all very weak evidence compared with the clear parallels with Luke's actual Gospel in Mark 12:32 and 12:34, quoted above.

(3) The Death of the Baptist (Mark 6:20-21). We can take as our third example one which has no parallel in Luke such as the first example had, and no Lucan connection in its context, as had the second. Boismard cites the following as Lucanisms:

Mark 6:20 : the word "man" ἀνήρ is "typical" of the style of Luke : 8/4/27/7/100; with a double qualification, as here in "a righteous and holy man," it occurs elsewhere only in Luke (7 times) and Acts (29 times).

Mark 6:21 : "make a dinner," which occurs only twice elsewhere (Luke 14:12, 16).

Mark 6:21 : "chiliarch" (ERV "high captain") : 0/1/0/1/17/2; "notable" or "chief" πρῶτος (in this sense) : 0/1/1/0/3.

---

[30]Farmer, *The Synoptic Problem*, 421.

Words are used of course not merely because they are favorites, but because the subject matter requires them. Luke has "make a dinner" twice, in close proximity (14:12, 16); having used the phrase once, he could hardly avoid its repetition. The only significance in the phrase "a righteous and holy man" could come from its use of two adjectives; "man" (ἀνήρ) is common enough, as is shown by the figures quoted. The one example which at first sight looks impressive is the use of the word "chiliarch" (ERV "chief/high captain"; NRSV "officer/tribune") which occurs seventeen times in Acts. The seventeen instances all occur in Acts 21:31–25.23; they are inevitable because of the subject matter; sixteen of them refer to the same person, and when he has once been so called no other title was possible. The last instance (Acts 25:23) is in the plural. The seventeen instances in effect really only come down to two.

Of course if Mark, as I submit, was dependent on Luke and not Luke on Mark, reminiscences of Lucan words or phrases may occur. It is noteworthy that Luke uses the word "chiliarch" accurately for the military tribune; Mark uses it more vaguely for a "high officer," which hardly suggests a Lucan hand. It is only if it is assumed that Luke depends on Mark, or on Boismard's Intermediate-Mark, that any problem arises from Lucan usages being reflected in Mark's text.

Just as Boismard sees a Lucan redaction of Mark, he also asserts that "the existence of an ultimate redaction of Mark, distinct from Intermediate-Mark, is also proved by the passages in Mark where one can disclose a Matthaean influence (Intermediate-Matthew).[31] He names as "one of the best examples" Mark 7:9-13 with its parallel in Matt 15:3-6.

Mark, inversely from Matthew, puts the argument of Jesus drawn from the Corban *after* the quotation of Isa 29:13. This argument seems an addition in Mark, introduced by the redactional "and he said to them" (v. 9a; cf. Bultmann, Dibelius); v. 9, belonging to the argumentation from the Corban, is moreover a doublet of v. 8, belonging to the argumentation from Isa 29:13. It is logical that if the argumentation from the Corban is a redaction of Intermediate-Matthew it would not have come into Mark except at the level of the last Marcan redaction.[32]

In the following verses of Mark, at the list of vices in 7:21-22,

Mark gives five of the six vices of the list of Intermediate-Matthew (Matt 15:19b), but adds a certain number of other vices, which have no relation to the precepts of the Decalogue: "coveting, wickedness, deceit, licentiousness, envy, slander, pride, foolishness." The passage from the plural (cf. Matthew) to the singular betrays a duality of sources.[33]

---

[31]Boismard, *Synopse*, 2:24.
[32]Boismard, *Synopse*, 2:230.
[33]Boismard, *Synopse*, 2:233.

As with the alleged Lucan redaction of Mark, the difficulties Boismard sees are created by his own theory of a multiplicity of sources. There is no problem if Mark depends on the canonical Matthew, just as other problems cease when we realize his dependence also on Luke. Mark's alterations are easily accounted for in the passage quoted if we recognize that they come from his own editorial hand. the section in Matthew is clearly more "primitive" and is marked by its Semitic inclusion: it begins with the question why the disciples transgress "for they wash not their hands when they eat bread," and it closes with "to eat with unwashed hands defileth not the man." In Matthew the references to washing is expected to be clear to the readers; Mark adds a long explanation (7:3-4) about its meaning. If these verses of Mark had been in Matthew and not in Mark, critic after critic would have cited them as proof of Mark's priority. They point instead to that of Matthew.

We must now turn to an argument in a book by M. D. Goulder.[34] It is Goulder's thesis that Matthew is a midrashic expansion of Mark, and he regards the priority of Mark as proved on statistical evidence. He works from the number of characteristic Matthaean words in the passages where "Matthew is usually believed to be overwriting Mark." The percentages he gives are as follows:

(1) Overall in the Matthaean passages: about fifteen percent.
(2) In the actual words Matthew and Mark have in common: about three percent.
(3) In the words they do not have in common: twenty-eight percent.

On grounds that had Mark used Matthew and copied Matthew's words the percentage of these groups would be about the same (that is, fifteen percent), Goulder concludes "therefore Marcan priority is true."[35] This conclusion however does not follow, except on the implied assumption that in following Matthew Mark would have copied his exact words. I offer two examples.

In Mark 1:16-20, parallel to Matt 4:18-22, Mark tells exactly the same story of the call of four disciples, only adding that Zebedee was left "with the hired men," but Mark does not reproduce all Matthew's words (or, alternatively, if Mark wrote first, Matthew does not reproduce all Mark's), and some variants are so slight as not to survive translation into English. Matthew, for example, twice has "they followed him"; Mark uses the phrase once, and on the second occasion varies it to "they went after him," having departed from Matthew's text by inserting "Zebedee in the boat with the hired men."

There is a wider variation of wording in a passage such as Mark 6:1-6 (Matt 13:53-58), the Rejection at Nazareth, where again a close parallel with Luke is

---

[34]*Midrash and Lection in Matthew*, Speaker's Lectures in Biblical Studies 1969–1971 (London: SPCK, 1974).
[35]Ibid., 122-23.

not in question, but the substance of the two accounts is the same. It is at least as easy to see Mark's version as dependent on Matthew as to see the reverse, and indeed there is good reason to regard Mark as secondary when he expands "And he did not many mighty works there, because of their unbelief" to "And he did not many mighty works there, save that he laid his hand upon a few sick folk, and healed them. And he marvelled because of their unbelief." It has been common to say that Matthew has altered Mark's "could not" to "did not" to avoid phrases "which seem to ascribe inability to Christ," but in fact Matthew's words imply the same meaning as Mark's: it was the faith of the people, not the power of Christ, that was lacking. It is Mark who softens the impact by his insertion of a few healings.

Goulder himself dispenses with the Q hypothesis, but as soon as one does that and gets away from the theory that the bulk of Matthew and Luke consists of Mark plus Q, the whole case for Marcan priority comes into serious question.

The question did receive serious consideration in 1964 in William R. Farmer's *The Synoptic Problem*, but it will be convenient before considering this to refer to a later book, John Drury's *Tradition and Design in Luke's Gospel*,[36] in which Goulder's thesis is carried a stage further. On the assumption made by Goulder that Matthew is a midrashic amplification of Mark, Drury proceeds further to argue that Luke used both Matthew and Mark, together with the Septuagint, and used the same midrashic method to compose his own Gospel. Drury might perhaps concede that Luke had other sources, though he never seems to suggest them.[37] Drury represents the first two chapters of Luke as being a Lucan creation, a midrash on Old Testament themes, the clue to this being largely the Septuagintal style and language Luke unquestionably uses, with the hints of Matthew 1 providing Luke's starting point. To argue from Luke's biblical style to such a conclusion is to make a serious leap in logic. It assumes that no other sources were at Luke's disposal. It assumes, for example, that the name Joseph only came from Matthew: "Luke takes Matthew's Joseph for granted in more senses than one," Matthew having given "the name of the great dreamer of the old dispensation for the dreamer of the new (Matt 1:20; 2:13; 2:13; 2:19), with a midrashic aptness which casts some doubt on its historicity";[38] whereas John 1:45 and 6:42 are clear indications of the existence of a tradition independent of Matthew. Again, for Drury the Magnificat and Benedictus are "certainly from the same hand which wrote the whole of the first two chapters,"[39]

---

[36]*Tradition and Design in Luke's Gospel: A Study in Early Christian Historiography* (London: Darton, Longman & Todd, 1976; Atlanta: John Knox Press, 1977).

[37]On Luke 19:1-10 Drury comments: "There may still be contributions from elsewhere" (ibid., 73), but goes on to derive them from Mark, Matthew or Q, and the Septuagint.

[38]Ibid., 123.

[39]Ibid., 49-50.

whereas their actual position in Luke's text, and particularly the absence of the
Benedictus immediately after 1:64, show that they were not, to use Drury's word,
"internal"[40] to the narrative of Luke 1 and 2. The place in Luke's text of such
passages as 3:23-38, 4:16-30, and 5:1-11 are clear indications of the way in
which he keeps different sources apart. We can only wonder whether Theophilus
would have been satisfied to think he was being led to the certainty of the things
of which he had been informed if he knew what a free hand Luke had exercised.

That Luke had other sources additional to or overlapping with what he found
in Matthew (or, in Drury's view, Mark) can be illustrated many times. I take
three examples.

(1) Luke 5:1-11; Mark 1:16-20; Matt 4:18-22. According to Drury, Mark's
calling of fishermen to discipleship "is Luke's Christian source," and Luke has
"made Mark's laconic statement about fishers of men into a tableau at Luke 5:1-
11,"[41] apparently only by drawing on suggestions from Old Testament stories.
Luke certainly uses his own story instead of that in Matthew and Mark, but
because it comes from a different source he does not include it in the same place.
But the obvious comparison with Luke's narrative is not with the passages in
Matthew and Mark, but with John 21:1-8. John's story of the miraculous catch
of fish is set after the Resurrection, and there may be more than one view as to
the connection of the two stories: both deal with great catches of fish, both deal
with scenes in the morning, and both lead on to the commission of Peter. What
is certain from the existence of the story in John 21 is that there was a tradition
of one and possibly two such episodes, and that it did not go back to Luke's
fertile mind brooding over the Old Testament. John 21 is not a midrash on Mark.

(2) Luke 12:49-53; Matt 10:34-36. The second example is one where there
are parallels between Luke and Matthew but not with Mark. It is a case where
Luke is aware of a source that overlaps with Matthew. Luke has "I came to cast
fire upon the earth . . . think not that I have come to give peace in the earth."
Matthew does not include the reference to fire, but has "Think not that I came
to cast peace upon the earth: I came not to cast peace, but a sword." Drury sees
allusions in Luke to Deuteronomy, and to "Elijah's fire raising." Both are
unnecessary. Matthew does not have the reference to fire, and therefore his
phrase "to cast peace" is as unexplained as it is peculiar. M.-J. Lagrange, who
saw the difficulty, was reduced to saying of the word "cast" (βαλεῖν), "the verb
has probably been used with εἰρήνη because it had been chosen for μάχαιρα,"[42]
but it is as inappropriate to a sword as to peace. Luke avoids it, but his record
of a fuller tradition, with the words "to cast fire," explains Matthew's wording.
Luke clearly has a source other than Matthew, though overlapping with him.

---

[40]Ibid., 50.

[41]Ibid., 74.

[42]Marie Joseph Lagrange, *Évangile selon saint Matthieu*, 7th ed. (Paris: Lecoffre,
1948; [1]1923) in loc.

Luke adds a further section about misunderstanding the time, also not dependent for its wording on Matthew (Luke 12:54-46; cf. Matt 16:2-3) before adding another short excerpt from Matthew's Sermon on the Mount (12:57-59; Matt 5:25-26).

(3) Luke 16:1-9. My third example is a narrative without parallel in either Matthew or Mark, the parable of the Unjust Steward. On the strength of the occurrence of the word φρόνιμος ("wise") in Luke 16:8 and of its occurrence seven times in Matthew, Drury supposes a Matthaean connection;[43] apart from this he holds that "the Old Testament provided the only adequate accessible solution to the problem of the source of a peculiarly Lucan parable"[44]—and this surprisingly in the story of the Samaritan lepers in 2 Kings 7. We need however to look more closely at Luke's text, which has unusual features. We find the Semitic form ὁ οἰκονόμος τῆς ἀδικίας (literally, "the steward of unrighteousness") in 16:8, just as there is ὁ κριτὴς τῆς ἀδικίας in 18:6 for the unrighteous judge in another peculiarly Lucan parable. In 16:9 the similar "mammon of unrighteousness" occurs, though in 16:11 "the unrighteous mammon" follows in more natural Greek. The Semitic usage must have come from Luke's source. Moreover, Luke uses the Jewish words "bath" and "cor" (both translated "measure" in ERV and RSV) although they are commonly translated into Greek in the Septuagint.[45] If Luke had been following Septuagintal usage, it would have been uncharacteristic for him to have used these forms; he was not writing for Palestinians. The simple explanation is that Luke had a special source. The same source is likely to have been responsible for "the sons of this age" and "the sons of light" in Luke 16:8: the phrases are not natural Greek usage.

In each of these passages the evidence points to Luke's having had access to sources now lost, not to his having composed a free midrash from the Old Testament or Matthew.

Turning from these false trails, we come back to William R. Farmer. The history of source criticism was reviewed by Farmer in *The Synoptic Problem*, and he came down decisively for the Griesbach hypothesis, that Mark wrote subsequently to, and made use of both Matthew and Luke. I believe he made his case. Although it has not yet been generally accepted, there are now frequent signs of doubt or at least of caution, among writers on the Gospels as to the validity of the Marcan-priority hypothesis. Not long before Farmer's book was published, Étienne Trocmé could write of the Griesbach hypothesis: "As a theory, it is not worth confuting."[46] But now, for example, John A. T. Robinson has noted:

---

[43]Drury, *Tradition and Design in Luke's Gospel*, 159.

[44]Ibid., 79.

[45]Although Ezra 7:22 has βατῶν and κόριον and Ezek 45:14 and 2 Chron 2:10 have κορῶν.

[46]*The Formation of the Gospel according to Mark*, trans. Pamela Gaughan (London: SPCK; Philadelphia: Westminster Press, 1975; French original, 1963) 10.

The consensus frozen by the success of "the fundamental solution" propounded
by Streeter has begun to show signs of cracking. Though this is still the domi-
nant hypothesis, encapsulated in the textbooks, its conclusions can no longer be
taken for granted as among the "assured results" of biblical criticism.[47]

It is not necessary here to reproduce Farmer's arguments; but as the significance
of verbal agreement between the Gospels can often be understood in contrary
ways and the acid test is often to be applied by considering the order of the
Gospel narratives the result of this will be apparent when we consider in the next
chapter the order of Luke's Gospel. The evidence relevant to the purpose of this
study will be seen to corroborate Farmer's thesis. For the present, some summary
comments must suffice.

It is indeed a great merit of Farmer's book that he sees the importance of
order in the Synoptics. Mark, he points out, "tends to agree more closely with
Matthew when they follow an order different from Luke, but more closely with
Luke when they follow an order different from Matthew."[48] This is capable of
a natural explanation if Mark is the third of the evangelists to write, and Farmer
has shown how natural is the order in Mark if he is conflating the accounts of
Matthew and Luke. Farmer does not himself deal with what is logically a prior
question, as to the order of the narrative in Luke if he is using Matthew. To this
we must turn our attention shortly.

At an important stage in his argument Farmer bases his case on "isolable and
objectively definable categories of literary phenomena":[49] on that of order and
content in the three Gospels; on the so-called minor agreements of Matthew and
Luke against Mark, taking into account that their agreements consist not only of
verbal identities, but also of omissions in common; and on the evidence that

> when Matthew and Mark are following the same order, but Luke exhibits a dif-
> ferent order, the texts of Matthew and Mark tend to be very close to one
> another. And when Luke and Mark are following the same order, but Matthew
> exhibits a different order, the texts of Luke and Mark tend to be very close to
> one another.[50]

The hypothesis of Marcan priority does not cover these facts; they are accounted
for, as Farmer has shown, if Mark made use of Matthew and Luke.

Farmer's insight in this matter is important as showing that Mark's project
in conflating Matthew and Luke did not constitute a task so difficult as to be

---

[47]*Redating the New Testament* (London: SCM; Philadelphia: Westminster Press, 1976)
93.

[48]Farmer, *The Synoptic Problem*, 211.

[49]Ibid.

[50]Ibid., 218.

improbable, as it has sometimes been alleged to be. The point is succinctly made by E. P. Sanders:

> If Mark had conflated Matthew and Luke, he would not have had to analyze their common matter and labor to include it. He could simply have copied first one then the other, thereby automatically including what was common to them, excluding any chance that they would agree together against him, and also creating agreements with each of them against the other.[51]

There is a further point of significance that strongly supports Farmer's thesis. There are parallel accounts in Matthew and Mark, not represented in Luke, that are so similar it is certain one is derived from the other. An example would be Matt 4:18-22 || Mark 1:16-20, the Call of the First Disciples. Similarly there are parallel accounts in Mark and Luke, not present in Matthew, where the same conclusion is inevitable. The story of the Widow's Offering, Mark 12:41-44 || Luke 21:1-4, is a case in point. Conversely, there are passages paralleled in all three Synoptics, with connections between Mark and each of the others, where neither of these keeps so closely to the wording or the details of the Marcan text. The long passage Matt 17:1-23 || Mark 9:2-32 || Luke 9:28-45 is of this kind. There are often correspondences, including omissions, that would be explicable if Luke used both Matthew and Mark, but the fundamental difficulty would remain if this hypothesis were accepted: why should Matthew sit more lightly to Mark's text when using passages which, though he would not have known it, Luke was going to use? And why should Luke sit more lightly to Mark's text when using passages that Matthew used? Mark has connections with both Matthew and Luke, and the problem disappears when it is assumed not that both used Mark, but that Mark used both of them, so variations from either occurred when he made use of the other.

Without repeating Farmer's argumentation, we may note there are frequent minor points that confirm his view and reveal the secondary character of Mark as against Matthew and Luke. The following are some examples.

(1) Mark 10:27 (Matt 19:26; Luke 18:27).

> With men it is impossible, but not with God;
> for all things are possible with God.

Charles F. Burney comments on this: "Clearly the addition [but not with God] is a gloss,"[52] on the ground that it breaks the parallelism in Matthew and Luke.

---

[51]*The Tendencies of the Synoptic Tradition*, SNTSMS 9 (London: Cambridge University Press, 1969).

[52]*Poetry of Our Lord*, 75n.1.

(2) Mark 8:15 (Matt 16:25; Luke 9:24).

> For whoever would save his life will lose it,
> and whoever loses his life for my sake and the gospel's will save it.

Burney says: "Mark adds 'and the gospel's' which clearly overweights the clause." He might also have connected this with another verse, Mark 13:10:

> And to all nations first must the gospel be preached,

which he finds "imperfectly rhythmical," and which also reflects the Marcan usage of "the gospel" in an absolute sense that does not occur in Matthew or Luke. Matthew once has "this gospel" (14:9) and is followed by Mark; elsewhere Matthew has "the gospel of the kingdom." Luke only uses the word "gospel" twice, both times in Acts: "the word of the gospel" (15:7) and "the gospel of the grace of God" (20:24). Mark's usage is clearly secondary and, when the word "gospel" is put without qualification in the words of Jesus, anachronistic.

(3) Mark 2:27.

> The sabbath was made for man, and not man for the sabbath.

The reference to "man" does not lead naturally to "so the Son of man is Lord also of the sabbath." In Matthew "something greater than the temple is here" (12:6). Mark has been following Luke, and has inserted this sentence through its verbal, but not logical, similarity.

(4) Mark 5:14. In the story of the Gerasene swine Mark gives their number as "about two thousand," a herd as unmanageable as it is unlikely. On form-critical grounds this betrays the secondary character of Mark as against Matthew and Luke. It may have arisen as a deduction from the word "legion": the Roman legion did not consist of two thousand men, but Mark may have thought so.

(5) Mark 3:14ff.

> And he appointed twelve that they might be with him . . .
> and he appointed the twelve, and Simon he surnamed Peter.

The difficulties of the text (reflected in the manuscripts) have as their most probable explanation the conflation of Matt 10:1ff. and Luke 6:12ff.

(6) Mark 9:41.

> In the name that ye are Christ's.

Matthew has "in the name of a disciple" (10:42). Dennis Nineham comments: "The word Christ is nowhere else in the Gospels or Acts used as a proper name without the article. So it seems clear that in its present form the phrase must be the work of the early Church."[53] The "early Church" here is the editor Mark, reflecting a later usage than Matthew's text.

---

[53]Nineham, *The Gospel of St. Mark*, in loc.

(7) Mark 13:18.

And pray ye that it be not in the winter.

The warning in Mark's "apocalypse" is paralleled in Matt 24:20, which adds "neither on a sabbath." J. A. T. Robinson calls it "one of those points of difference where, unless one is committed to overall Marcan priority, it looks as though Mark has omitted an element in the tradition no longer relevant for the Gentile church."[54]

(8) Mark 14:65 (Matt 26:67-68; Luke 22:63-64). Matthew has "Then did they spit in his face, and struck him, and some slapped him, saying, Prophesy unto us, thou Christ; who is he that struck thee?" Luke makes the question more intelligible by saying "And the men that held him mocked him and beat him, and they blindfolded him, and asked him, saying, Who is he that struck thee?" Mark takes up Luke's blindfolding: "And some began to spit on him, and to cover his face," but reduces the words of the tormentors to simply "Prophesy." He has conflated Matthew and Luke, but neglected to make clear the purpose of the blindfolding.

Examples such as these are not individually conclusive of Mark's having followed Matthew and Luke, but taken together they are significant as supporting the Griesbach hypothesis. It will be reinforced as we, in later chapters, we follow Luke's method.

The primary test of the Griesbach hypothesis lies in the order which is to be seen in the three Synoptics, and to this, at least so far as it concerns the Third Gospel, we shall turn in a later chapter. It has been well said that "if then we find that the comparison of the sequence patterns reveals the clear dependence of one Gospel on another, and of the third on the two former, we may reasonably argue that we have discovered the relative chronological sequence of the three Synoptic Gospels (though not yet of their true date)."[55] It is to this question that we shall have to return. In the meantime, the following examples may be given to show how the Griesbach hypothesis can illuminate the texts.

(1) Matthew 3:7-10; Luke 3:7-9. There is here a passage of no fewer then sixty-three words in Matthew that are reproduced in Luke with only three modifications. In Luke 3:9 the word καί ("also") is added, and in 3:8 Matthew's "fruit" is put into the plural and the word ἄρξησθε ("begin") replaces Matthew's δόξητε ("think"). If we take into account that both evangelists impress their own styles on their writing, it would be remarkable that, supposing they were using a common text, both should on this occasion have followed it so closely. It is much less remarkable if it is only one who is copying the other. Of Luke's three

---

[54]Robinson, *Redating the New Testament*, 23.

[55]J. Bernard Orchard, "J. A. T. Robinson and the Synoptic Problem," *New Testament Studies* 22/3 (April 1976): 352.

alterations, one (the addition of καί) is of little significance. The phrase "begin to say" is typical of Luke's style (for example, 11:29; 12:1) and he may well have regarded Matthew's "Do not think to say to yourselves" (literally "in yourselves") as tautological and equivalent to "do not think to think." If Luke copied Matthew, both the close correspondence of the long passage and the slight alterations are easily accounted for. There are other passages to which similar considerations apply.

(2) Matthew 13:55; Mark 6:3; Luke 4:23. Where Matthew has "Is not this the son of the carpenter?" Mark has "Is not this the carpenter?" and Luke has "Is not this the son of Joseph?" If Mark were the source of the other two Gospels, it is not clear what Matthew has gained by putting "the son of the carpenter" nor why, unless Luke knew Matthew, he should make a similar alteration to "the son of Joseph." But if Matthew came first, it is completely natural for Luke to write "the son of Joseph," whom he has already named in the childhood stories and in the genealogy and, incidentally, without saying he was a carpenter. Mark's alteration, if he knew Luke's Gospel, is also entirely natural: as he has not included the record of Jesus' virginal conception, of which he must have been aware, he would therefore be open to misunderstanding if he wrote "the son of the carpenter." That Mark did not include the Infancy narratives certainly does not imply he did not accept them as true. The Griesbach hypothesis is the simplest explanation of the facts.

(3) Matthew 26:64; Mark 14:62; Luke 22:67-70. The answer of Jesus to the high priest's question "Art thou the Christ?" is given in a significantly different form in Mark as against Matthew and Luke. According to Mark, Jesus answered "I am; and ye shall see the Son of man sitting at the right hand of power, and coming with the clouds of heaven." In his study of the doctrine of the parousia, John A. T. Robinson comments as follows on the texts of Matthew and Luke:

> We are struck at once by the fact that in each of them there is introduced a qualifying phrase, putting beyond doubt that what they prescribe is "from this moment." In Matt 26 it is "from now on you will see the Son of man sitting at the right hand of Power, and coming in the clouds of heaven," and in Luke 22:69: "From now on the Son of man shall be seated at the right hand of the power of God." This concurrence between the two evangelists is remarkable, if both were using Mark independently.[56]

Robinson goes on to point out that there are two other agreements between Matthew and Luke over against Mark. Whereas Mark has the direct answer to the high priest's question "Art thou the Christ?" Matthew and Luke record an evasive answer (as all three do in recording Jesus' answer to Pilate: Matt 27:11; Mark 15:2; Luke 23:3); and both have a "but" between the two halves of Jesus'

---

[56]*Jesus and His Coming: The Emergence of a Doctrine* (New York: Abingdon Press; London: SCM, 1957) 47-48.

reply. Robinson, who in his *Jesus and His Coming* assumed the priority of Mark, makes the tentative interpretation of the evidence that originally Mark wrote "*You have said that* I am, *but from now on* you shall see," and so forth. Robinson would of course have agreed that this is only a conjecture (and indeed he was later less likely to regard it as satisfactory than when he wrote in 1957), but in fact the difficulty disappears if we recognize that Luke is dependent on Matthew, and that Mark has abbreviated their text: for "from now on" Luke has ἀπὸ τοῦ νῦν as against Matthew's ἀπ' ἄρτι, "changing the Greek phrase," as Robinson says, "in accordance with his regular stylistic preference." Mark expands "the power" as a name of God to "the power of God" as a more natural phrase for his readers.

If then, as I hold, Griesbach's hypothesis is correct, questions inevitably arise concerning each of the three Synoptics. Matthew then is certainly not a midrashic expansion of Mark, and the date of Matthew calls for reconsideration. If Matthew represents the final form of a gradually extended Gospel, indeed possibly with an Aramaic Gospel by the apostle Matthew in the background but developed by a "school of Matthew"[57] at more than one stage and even conceivably (as Farmer tentatively suggested) the narrative that "many had taken in hand" to which Luke refers, it may be true that there were elements in the ultimate text not present when Luke wrote. Matthew, as John A. T. Robinson said, "could therefore in a real sense turn out to be both the earliest and the latest of the Synoptists."[58] The text itself gives some indications of revision of greater or lesser extent. Of small additions, Stendahl for instance shows reason to regard Matt 12:40 and 13:14-15 "as interpretations at a later stage than that which in a true sense can be regarded as the period when the gospel came into being."[59]

As to Mark, Joseph B. Tyson in a valuable study discusses the possibility that Mark used Matthew and Luke, and of that hypothesis writes:

> Perhaps the major problem which may be raised relates to Mark's failure to use some 33-36 pericopes which he found in both Matthew and Luke. The study of sequential parallelism suggests that he omitted them because they were in variant sequences in his sources. Mark used almost everything which exhibited sequential parallelism in his sources. To be sure, he used some nonsequential material from both his sources, but he had a decided preference for material on the sequence of which his sources agreed. In fact, he used 91% of the sequen-

---

[57]Cf. Krister Stendahl, *The School of St. Matthew and Its Use of the Old Testament*, Acta Seminarii neotestamentici Upsaliensis 20, 2nd ed. (Lund: Gleerup, 1968; Philadelphia: Fortress Press, 1968; ¹1954).

[58]*Redating the New Testament*, 102.

[59]Stendahl, *The School of Matthew*, 135.

tially parallel material he found in Matthew and Luke, and retained the
sequence of all of it.[60]

To recognize that Luke used Matthew (and that Mark used both Matthew
and Luke) does not necessarily imply that the text of Matthew available to the
other evangelists was identical with what we now have as the canonical Gospel.
I have argued elsewhere, in *The Making of Mark* and more fully in *The First
Gospel*, that the present text of Matthew is a development of a shorter "Proto-
Matthew" to which the Infancy stories of the first two chapters and the closing
passage of 28:9-20 together with other material within the body of the Gospel are
the additions of a later editor to the original and very early text. As concerns
Luke, we have to try to understand the working of his mind, on the assumption
that we have only one earlier text with which to compare his Gospel, the Gospel
of Matthew. The test of that assumption must be found primarily in the order of
Luke's Gospel.

---

[60]"Parallelism in the Synoptic Gospels," *New Testament Studies* 22/3 (April 1976):
292.

Chapter 3

The Order of the Gospel

To write unto thee in order. . . .   —Luke 1:3

The study of the order followed in Luke's Gospel provides a test for the thesis that Matthew is a source—indeed the only extant source—used by Luke, but it also gives insight into the special purpose of the evangelist. In following the development of the Gospel's order it is possible to enter into the working of the author's own mind as he selected and arranged the material he needed.

Even in its broad outline—Infancy, Ministry, and Passion—the Third Gospel is similar to Matthew. From our familiarity with the four Gospels it is easy to make an unconscious assumption that there is an inevitable "gospel form." Because John, as well as the Synoptists, includes a Passion narrative, it may be easy to overlook that John has a very different structure from the other three Gospels. And since the Synoptics are closely interrelated, with Mark as it were truncated at its beginning and end as compared with Matthew and Luke, it is easy to assume that there was a pattern which would inevitably suggest itself to anyone writing a "gospel." But if we recognize that Mark is dependent on Matthew and Luke, and Luke itself dependent on Matthew, we can see that it is Matthew who has given us the form with which we are familiar, and that this was in itself a remarkable achievement. Matthew himself was not writing pure biography, following the course of a life through its chronological order; he was proclaiming the "gospel" and arranging his material to that end. As I have argued elsewhere (in *The First Gospel*), the text of Matthew available to Luke was probably without the first two chapters of the canonical text, but allowing for this, Luke (like Mark) had a model for a book dealing with the Ministry of Jesus from the time of his Baptism by John and continuing with the story of his Passion to the proclamation of his Resurrection. Luke did not choose to follow Matthew's arrangement of the Ministry and Teaching (possibly suggested by the five books of Moses), but the broad outline was already provided for him.

On this basic plan, Luke himself tells us how he planned his work. he wrote his first volume to show "all that Jesus began both to do and to teach, until the day that he was taken up" (Acts 1:1), and it is on this model that his Gospel is arranged. Following some introductory matters, including the Infancy narrative (1:1–3:37), Luke proceeds to tell of "all that Jesus began to do" (4:1–9:50); he then concentrates on what "Jesus began to teach" (9:51–21:38); and finally, in his narrative of the Passion, Resurrection, and Ascension, he relates the events culminating with "the day that he was taken up" (22:1–24:52). In the words of the risen Christ Luke also discloses the plan of his second volume, as the record of the witness to the Gospel "in Jerusalem and in all Judæa and Samaria, and unto the end of the earth" (Acts 1:8): in Jerusalem where his first volume closed (Acts 1:1–8:3); in Judæa and Samaria (8:4–12:25); and finally to the secular capital of the known world, Rome, as representing "the end of the earth" (13:1–28:31).

We have then a broad division of Luke's Gospel into four parts, which necessarily entailed some rearrangement of the Matthaean material and also allowed for contributions from other sources available to the author. We have to consider each of these four parts in turn.

The Introduction

Matthew has already provided the idea of an introductory section. Comparison with Mark has very naturally created the impression that Matthew's introductory section consists of only the first two chapters, dealing with the Infancy of Jesus. And Matthew's collection of so much of Jesus' teaching in five great discourses has suggested these discourses are the basis of his whole structure. It has however forcibly been argued by Jack Dean Kingsbury[1] that the overall arrangement of Matthew is not dependent on the five discourses with their similar conclusions ("And when Jesus had finished these sayings . . . ," 8:1; cf. 11:1; 13:53; 19:1; 26:1), which are commonly understood as the controlling element in his arrangement, but is to be found in a threefold division. The scheme may be set out as follows.

1. The Coming of the Son of God (1:1–4:16).
2. The Proclamation of the Son of God (4:17–16:20).
3. The Suffering, Death, and Resurrection of the Son of God (16:21–28:20).

The clue to this arrangement is found, not in the parallel words that close the five discourses, but in the parallel words that open the second and third sections:

Matt 4:17 From that time began Jesus to preach, and to say, Repent ye; for the kingdom of heaven is at hand.
Matt 16:21 From that time began Jesus to show unto his disciples that he must go unto Jerusalem, and suffer many things of the elders and chief priests and scribes, and be killed, and the third day be raised up.

---

[1] In his *Matthew: Structure, Christology, Kingdom* (Philadelphia: Fortress Press; London: SPCK, 1976).

Whether Luke recognized this as the general structure of Matthew may be doubted, but he does not limit his own introduction to the first two chapters, with their account of Jesus' infancy. Luke's first section extends from the announcing of the coming birth of John as the forerunner of Jesus to the fulfillment of John's work in the Baptism of Jesus. Indeed all that Luke has to record about John (apart from the witness of Jesus about him in the course of his Ministry, in 7:18-35 and 16:16), his birth, his relationship to Jesus, his preaching, his baptizing Jesus, and his imprisonment, is included in this introduction. For Jesus himself, Luke begins with the announcing of his coming, then relates his birth and up-bringing as a faithful son of Israel and his baptism when there came to him who was to be "called holy, the Son of God" the voice of the Father saying "Thou art my beloved Son" (3:22).

The influence of Matthew 16;21 may however be seen in the way Luke begins a major section of his own Gospel at 9:51. That section is dedicated to Jesus' teaching, but from its beginning, and especially in the opening words, the thought that Jesus "must go to Jerusalem" is kept before the reader.

Matthew's Gospel begins with the genealogy of Jesus, which is followed by the story of his birth and that of the Magi and the Flight into Egypt. This is, I believe, an addition made later to the Matthaean text available to Luke. Luke has an independent account of Jesus' birth that shows no acquaintance with the story of the Magi, which is integral to Matthew's narrative as showing how Jesus, born in the city of David in Judæa (though the place is not recorded in chapter 1) came to live in Nazareth in Galilee. In dealing with the birth of Jesus, the primary purpose both of Matthew and Luke is to show Jesus' Davidic descent of which Bethlehem, the place of his birth, was an appropriate symbol. But whereas Matthew sets out to show how Jesus, born at Bethlehem, came to live at Nazareth, Luke conversely has to show how Jesus, whose mother belonged to Nazareth, came to be born at Bethlehem. Luke had clearly abundant material about the infancy of Jesus independently of Matthew, and used what was relevant to his own purpose.

While Matthew begins his Gospel with the genealogy of Jesus, Luke begins with the announcement of the birth of the Baptist. Luke has an independent form of the genealogy, and according to his usual custom when he changes from one source to another, he does not insert it into the midst of other material but appends it as the final item. Matthew's first chapter has a Genesis motif, and Genesis was not far from Luke's own thoughts for he carries the genealogy of Jesus, "being, as was supposed, the son of Joseph," through in the end to "the son of Adam, the son of God."

Matthew's genealogy is an artificial construction, as Matthew himself makes clear. Matthew's genealogy is at pains to carry the connection through the royal line, through Solomon to David, and its contents are influenced by the text of the first of the books of Chronicles which, Jeremias has reminded us, "even in

Palestine were included in the canon only in the course of the first century A.D."[2]
The form Luke had is more likely to go back to a family tradition, which makes
no claim to descent from David through a royal line, and it seems to be
preferable to Matthew's for the postexilic period. Jeremias's judgment, for
example, is that "we shall not hesitate to assume that Luke, or his source, may
have preserved authentic material, at least for the last few generations before
Joseph."[3] It was from the period of the Exile that racial purity became a serious
concern in Israel, and written records were kept. For the construction of
genealogies going back before the Exile, recourse could only be had to statements in the Hebrew Bible or to family traditions. That Luke's list is based on
some written source is witnessed to by the one obvious error he makes for the
postexilic period: he inserts "Rhesa" in "the (son) of Joanan, the (son) of Rhesa,
the (son) of Zerubbabel," as against 1 Chron 3:19. "Rhesa" has been shown to
be merely the Aramaic word for "prince," and therefore originally inserted as a
title of Zerubbabel. It implies therefore that Luke was using a translation, and at
this point a mistranslation, of an Aramaic list.

What most concerns our immediate purpose is that Luke had access to what
he regarded as an accurate list, one which may well have been preserved in
Joseph's family. The Davidic descent, to which it is meant to give support, is
witnessed to in the New Testament, not only in the Gospels,[4] and does not seem
to have been challenged by Jesus' opponents. That Jesus was a "son of David"
was proclaimed as part of the validation of the claim that he was the Messiah.

Luke 1:5–2:52. The Birth Stories. There is no reason to suppose that Luke
was dependent on Matthew for anything in his first two chapters. It is unwarrant-
ed conjecture that "Luke has woven the Matthaean threads into his own fabric:
a tapestry made of Old Testament skeins."[5] Their points of contact and diver-
gence can be easily seen. To both, Jesus was born during the days of Herod the
king; his mother was called Mary, and she was married to Joseph who was a
descendent of David; the conception of Jesus was through the operation of the
Holy Spirit; his name "Jesus" was ordained by an angel; he was born at
Bethlehem but grew up at Nazareth; he came to save his people. So far there is
identity, but in Matthew it is Joseph to whom the name Jesus was announced;
in Luke it is to Mary. In Matthew, Jesus was "to save his people from their
sins"; in Luke the words "Saviour" (2:11) and "salvation" (1:69, 71) are used in
a more general sense. That Jesus came from Nazareth is independently stated by

---

[2]Joachim Jeremias, *Jerusalem in the Time of Jesus* (Philadelphia: Fortress Press;
London, 1969) 295.

[3]Ibid., 297.

[4]E.g., Rom 1:3; Heb 7:14; Rev 22:16.

[5]John Drury, *Tradition and Design in Luke's Gospel: A Study in Early Christian Historiography* (London: Darton, Longman & Todd, 1976; Atlanta: John Knox Press, 1977)
126.

John, and his birth at Bethlehem is characteristically alluded to in John 7:41; he was known as "the son of Joseph" (John 1:43), and his virgin birth is alluded to (or in the less commonly accepted form of the text, actually stated) in John 1:13 and probably in John 8:41. The Davidic descent is alluded to in John 7:42 (as also elsewhere in the New Testament). The Fourth Gospel, which mentions six (or if Nathanael is the same as Bartholomew, seven) of the twelve disciples but never uses the name of James and John, does not include the name of Mary, but only speaks of the "mother of Jesus," significantly, in view of John 19:27, where she is associated with "the disciple whom Jesus loved"; but there is no doubt that the Evangelist knew her name. There is therefore nothing in Luke's agreements with Matthew to suggest dependence on him; there is surely common tradition behind all three Gospels.

Luke indeed writes in the first two chapters in a free and continuous style, very much in the manner of the Septuagint, and it is probably that so far as literary form is concerned, he is not using any previous written document. It is impossible to say who was his immediate informant, but if Mary was present at the birth of John,[6] she was the one person who could be the ultimate source of all that is contained in these two chapters. It has often been noticed that these chapters relate the story from Mary's point of view. Luke himself twice says that she "kept all these things in her heart" (2:19, 51), and says that all who heard of the events of John's birth also "laid them up in their heart." As R. O. P. Taylor has written, "the point to be emphasized is the deliberate use of a phrase speaking of memorizing, and the consequent guarantee of Luke's insertion."[7]

In view of Luke's own statements, and indeed of his use of sources in the rest of the Gospel, it is quite unjustified to claim that Luke has just given rein to his imagination in his first two chapters. In his *Tradition and Design in Luke's Gospel* Drury writes: "One thing at least is clear: the midrashic use of the Old Testament gives so satisfactory an account of the origin of Luke 1 and 2 that there is no need to posit Christian sources—still less sources from the circle of John the Baptist."[8] On the contrary, let us take one instance—an example of the significance of the apparently insignificant. In Luke 2:36-37 there is the account of the widow Anna. Luke was certainly interested in widows, but that hardly means that they do not exist. He could have no conceivable theological reason for inventing a father Phanuel, nor for recording the incidental fact that Anna was of the tribe of Asher, nor for the details of her age. The only reason for giving these particulars must be that Luke believed them to be true. But the story of Anna cannot stand by itself; it is part of the story of the Presentation in the temple, and if the information about Anna came to Luke from a source, it must

---

[6]See 81, below.

[7]*The Groundwork of the Gospels with Some Collected Papers* (Oxford: Basil Blackwell, 1946) 110.

[8]P. 66.

follow that the story of the Presentation as a whole came from that source. The alternative would be that Luke was such a fiction writer that he could not possibly give his Christian readers any confidence about the things of which they had been instructed.

With two exceptions the narrative of the first two chapters forms such a coherent whole that it is natural to conclude that it was written by Luke on the basis of one source, which may of course have been oral. The two exceptions are the Magnificat, the song of Mary after the Annunciation, and the Benedictus, the song of Zacharias after John's birth. That they did not come to Luke as part of the material he used for these two chapters is shown by their position, for when Luke turns to a different source, with separate materials, he does not conflate his texts. To take the Benedictus first, had it been part of Luke's continuous narrative its obvious place would have been after 1:64: "And his mouth was opened immediately, and his tongue loosed, and he spake, blessing God." In fact, it is left over until the end of the narrative about John's birth, without any suggestion as to the precise moment when it was uttered, leaving only the final closing words of the dismissal[9] to be added: "And the child grew, and waxed strong in spirit, and was in the deserts till the day of his showing unto Israel." The same pattern is to be seen in the inclusion of the Magnificat (1:46-55). If this is removed from the text, the story of the Visitation is seen to be a shorter addendum to that of the Annunciation (as 1:24-25 is to the announcement to Zacharias), and after Elisabeth's greeting (1:42-45) the narrative continues naturally with 1:56: "And Mary abode with her about six months, and returned unto her house." As the song of Mary is not part of the continuous narrative Luke leaves it to the end of the story of the Annunciation and Visitation, again only leaving the characteristic words of dismissal to close the section.

Luke 3:1-39. The Baptist. Coming to the period of John's preaching, Luke has Matthew's text available, but first he marks the new beginning and notes its connection with what has already been related. As the birth of Jesus and of the Baptist was "in the days of Herod, king of Judæa," so now a new date is given, setting the scene in the political and religious context (3:1-2). This was the time when "the word of God came unto John the son of Zacharias in the wilderness" where he had waited "till the day of his showing unto Israel" (1:80). So Luke passes on to repeat what he found in Matthew, with two additions. In the first addition he extends the Matthaean quotation from Isaiah 40 to include the words "and all flesh shall see the salvation of God." Luke never forgets where his story is leading him. The second addition of the practical application of John's message (3:10-14) comes to Luke from a different source. He therefore keeps it back to add at the end of the Matthaean text of John's preaching, before the

---

[9]Regarding this device, see below, chap. 4.

words that contrast the baptism with water and the baptism with the Holy Spirit and with fire lead on to the record of Jesus himself being baptized.

Apart from these two additions Luke is following Matthew, and at this first point where he is doing so it is illuminating to observe his method. There is a distinction between the way he treats the spoken words and the narrative which enshrines them. For the spoken words, apart from small stylistic variants, Luke copies Matthew closely, almost word for word, but he clearly feels free to remodel the words of the narrative in his own style. In this narrative he substitutes the vaguer "crowd" for "many of the Pharisees and Sadducees" since their distinctive interests and tenets are not obvious at this point. When later Luke has to mention Pharisees (5:17) he speaks of "Pharisees and doctors of the law," the added phrase (used instead of "scribes") presumably to give his Gentile readers some idea about what sort of people the Pharisees were. And so far as possible Luke drops out all reference to the Sadducees, who were of no particular interest to his readers. When later Luke cannot avoid a reference to the Sadducees (20:27, the only instance in the Gospel) he defines the word: "they which say that there is no resurrection." Matt 22:23 has the rather different phrase: "Sadducees came, saying that there is no resurrection."

The introduction draws to its close with the reference to John's imprisonment and the record of Christ's own Baptism. Here the reader has reached the first of the three peaks in the Gospel landscape: the Baptism with the Father's voice saying "Thou art my beloved Son" as the seal of approval on Jesus' vocation; the Transfiguration with the voice from heaven saying "This is my Son" as the seal on his Ministry; and the Ascension at the close of the Gospel as the seal of his Passion. Then, before the story of the Ministry begins, Luke, as we have seen, appends the genealogy to close the section.

"All that Jesus began to do"

After the story of the Baptism Matthew continues with "Then Jesus was led up by the Spirit into the wilderness to be tempted by the devil" (Matt 4:1 NRSV). Luke, to whom the Temptation was the beginning of the account of Jesus' Ministry, extends this, with the significance of the Baptist in mind, to "Jesus, full of the Holy Spirit, returned from the Jordan and was led by the Spirit in the wilderness, where for forty days he was tempted by the devil" (Luke 4:1-2 NRSV). Luke's phrase avoids the interpretation that could be put on Matthew's, that the Holy Spirit led Jesus into temptation (cf. Matt 3:13: "to be baptized").

An obvious difference between Matthew's and Luke's texts is in the order of the temptations. The ground of temptation was in the significance of the title "Son of God," and Luke's rearrangement may have been in order to end the temptations with an inclusion, the first and last of the temptations in his order beginning "If thou art the Son of God." Luke's wording perhaps also provides a clue that he did not think of the three temptations in a naive way as isolated occasions when the devil visibly appeared in some form, but of the three types

of temptation which Jesus had to face in this period of preparation. That one of
the temptations is said by Luke to have been "in a moment of time" (4:5) may
be an indication of its visionary character as he saw it. As to the form of this
pericope, whereas Matthew ends with "angels came and ministered to him," Luke
ends with one of his dismissals: "And when the devil had completed every
temptation, he departed from him for a season" (ἄχρι καιροῦ; RSV "until an
opportune time," 4:13).

Luke 4:14-30. The Gospel Proclaimed. From the Temptation, Matthew
moves rapidly to the proclamation of Jesus' teaching in the Sermon on the
Mount. He prepares for it by recording that Jesus left Nazareth for Capernaum
and began to preach and to heal in Galilee, and called his first disciples. After
this brief introduction (Matt 4:12-25) he passes immediately to the first of his
five great discourses, each of which is a compilation of traditions of Jesus'
teaching. For Luke, the first thing to be done is to show "all that Jesus began to
do," concentrating on this, and reserving the fuller treatment of all that Jesus
began to teach for later inclusion. Luke must therefore begin differently from
Matthew, with Jesus indeed proclaiming the good news, but not yet with long
accounts of his teaching. Matthew himself has at a later point (13:53-58) a short
narrative of Jesus in the synagogue in "his own country"; for Luke it is convenient to bring this forward, since he has a fuller tradition from some other source
which supplies what he needs here and which enables him to start where Jesus
had lived hitherto, at Nazareth. It is significant that here, and here alone, Luke
uses the unusual form "Nazara," which he copies form Matt 4:13 (the only place
where Matthew uses it), for he is still keeping his eye on where he has got to in
Matthew's text. Then in an illuminating picture of synagogue worship at that
time, we are told of Jesus' reading of a lesson from Isaiah: "The Spirit of the
Lord is upon me" (connecting up again with the descent of the Spirit at his
Baptism), and the proclamation that the Scripture he has read is now fulfilled.

By narrating this episode at this point Luke has been able to serve three
purposes: he has set out a program for Jesus' ministry; he has pointed out its
character of fulfillment; and he has shown the first signs of something at which
he has already hinted: "Behold, this child is set for the falling and rising up of
many in Israel" (Luke 2:34). The significance of the rejection of Jesus and the
Christian gospel is something Luke has to deal with as part of his purpose in
writing. Already at Nazareth, the opposition to Jesus among his own people is
apparent. Luke will be recurring to it during the Galilean Ministry, in Jerusalem
and after, down to what are almost the final words of Acts: "Go thou unto this
people, and say, By hearing ye shall hear, and shall in no wise understand; and
seeing ye shall see, and shall in no wise perceive" (Acts 28:26).

Luke 4:31-42. Jesus at Capernaum. At the point where Luke turned from
Matthew's order (where the significant reading "Nazara" appears), Matthew was
speaking of Jesus going to Capernaum, and it is therefore to Capernaum that
Luke now turns. Already in the story of the rejection at Nazareth, he has had

perforce to refer to Capernaum (4:23) where Jesus had already been, but this was incidental to his following a thematic rather than a chronological order. Luke still wishes to leave the Sermon on the Mount for the present, and this naturally involves him in leaving over the events that Matthew relates at the end of the sermon, the healing of the leper and of the centurion's servant. The words of Luke 4:23 ("Whatsoever we have heard at Capernaum") lead in naturally to Luke's taking up Matthew's thread where he had left it, "leaving Nazara he came and dwelt at Capernaum" (Matt 4:13), and omitting Matthew's Call of the First Disciples, for which Luke proposes to substitute a narrative from a different tradition; he merely adds Matthew's comment at the end of the sermon, that Jesus spoke with authority (Matt 7:28-29; Luke 4:31-32). Luke is now ready to speak about Capernaum and the mission in Galilee.

Never assuming knowledge of the topography of Palestine in his readers, Luke introduces the town in his usual way: "Then he came down to Capernaum, a city of Galilee" (4:31). Assuming (no doubt correctly) that the teaching of which Matthew spoke was normally in the synagogue, and having from some other source a story of the exorcism of a man "having the spirit of an unclean demon" (4:31-37) which took place in the synagogue, Luke inserts this before returning to Matthew.

Because Luke has so far not been able to include the call of Peter, it is convenient for him to resume, in Matthew's accounts of Capernaum, not with the story of the centurion's servant, but with the healing of Peter's wife's mother, to lead into the story of Peter's call (just as the reference at Nazareth had led into dealing with Capernaum). The story of the healing therefore follows, with the healing at the close of the sabbath ("when the sun was setting") of many sick people. Then, in a note of his own, not taken from Matthew, Luke records that Jesus withdrew from Capernaum, saying that he must preach the gospel of the kingdom of God to the other cities also, and so closes this group of narratives with words suggested by Matthew's own conclusion before the Sermon on the Mount (Matt 4:22: "And he was preaching in the synagogues of Judæa" (Luke 4:44).[10] Luke seems fond of using such summaries.

Luke 5:1-11. The Call of Peter. So far Luke has covered all the material in Matthew as far as Matt 8:17 except for the Call of the First Disciples, Peter and his associates (omitted because Luke is to use an independent tradition) and the Sermon on the Mount with its two appended stories. The call of Peter is therefore now included, after the incidental introduction of his name in the phrase "Simon's wife's mother." Luke keeps very faithfully to his sources, even if the explanation of events or the identification of a person has to be delayed. He

---

[10]"Judæa" is used in the wider, generic sense; geographically it is still Galilee that is in question. The "Judæa" reading is explained thus in an NEB footnote: "Or *the Jewish synagogues*."

gives it as speedily as possible. Incidentally, he still refers to the disciple as
Simon, but in 5:8 speaks of Simon Peter, making the identification clear.

Luke 5:12-16. A Leper Healed. The story has developed naturally, from
preaching in Nazareth to preaching in the synagogues of Galilee, and before beginning a fresh theme, Luke finds it convenient to fill up one of the gaps in his
use of Matthew, the healing of a leper. In the sermon at Nazareth, Jesus had said
that there were many widows in Israel in the days of Elijah, who had only been
sent to Zarephath to a woman who was a widow. And in the days of Elisha there
were many lepers in Israel, but only Naaman the Syrian was cleansed. Elijah had
performed a miracle for a widow, of whom God had said, "Behold, I have com-
manded a widow there to feed thee" (1 Kings 17:9); and as Elijah had gone out
of Israel and performed the miracle for the woman who was to feed him, so now
Jesus had gone out of Nazareth (and no doubt there were many widows in Nazareth) and performed a miracle for Peter's wife's mother, who may well have
been a widow, and "she rose and served them." Elisha had healed a leper, and
Matthew provided an account of Jesus doing the same (Matt 8:1-4). In Matthew
the incident occurs when Jesus came down from the mount, and Luke, as he
completes the widow-leper parallel, is careful not to invent a different and definite context. He gives a vague one instead: "And it came to pass when he was
in one of the cities." The whole section closes with a dismissal, that "Jesus was
withdrawing in desert places and praying" (Luke 5:16); it would perhaps be more
naturally translated "Jesus used to withdraw to lonely places to pray."

Luke 5:17-26. The Paralytic. Luke then, apart from the Sermon on the
Mount with the following story of the centurion's servant, has used Matthew as
far as 8:17; but he now goes a little further before continuing from that point. He
has already recorded that Jesus preached at Nazareth and that even there, in his
home town, he had met opposition. As the story unfolds, Luke has to show that
the opposition with which his readers were familiar in the growing church was
already apparent in an area broader than Nazareth. Luke therefore takes two
separate groups of stories from Matthew (Matt 9:1-7; 12:1-15). It is the resultant
collection of five stories of conflict that has been supposed by critics holding the
hypothesis of Marcan priority to have been an existing collection incorporated
in Mark. If Luke used Matthew, there is no need to imagine such a document.

The first of these episodes is of the healing of a paralytic (5:17-26). Matthew
had given it a definite context: "And he entered a boat, and crossed over, and
came into his own city," that is, Capernaum; but Luke only wants the story for
its lesson and does not pretend to be putting it in a chronological order. So he
simply begins "And it came to pass on one of those days." As he is now dealing
with the wider mission of Jesus and with the opposition to it, he adds to Matthew's account that there were Pharisees and doctors of the law who had come
from "every village of Galilee and Judæa and Jerusalem"; in Matthew they are
only "certain scribes." They accused Jesus of blasphemy: "Who can forgive sins,

but God alone?" But the miracles of healing were signs of God at work, and the lesson for men was that "the son of man has authority on earth to forgive sins."

Luke 5:27-32. Publicans and Sinners. "After these things" (5:27)—a phrase Luke can use because he is now following Matthew's sequence—Luke goes on to the call of Levi. For Luke the point of the story is not that another of the Twelve was being called, but that Jesus would eat with tax collectors and sinners, those with whom the Pharisees "and their scribes" (a phrase Luke adds) would not join in table fellowship. To Matthew's ending "I have not come to call the righteous" Luke adds "to repentance."

Since Luke and Mark, apparently independently, have "Levi" where the First Gospel has "Matthew" it would appear probable that this is what they found in their copy of that Gospel ("Proto-Matthew"), and that an editor has wanted to make clear that Levi is the same as the Apostle Matthew. He appears to have emphasized this by adding "the tax collector" to Matthew's name in his list of apostles in Matt 10:3, an addition that does not appear in the lists of either Luke 2:15 or Mark 3:18 (or in Acts 1:13).

Luke 5:33-39. Fasting. Luke can still follow Matthew's sequence (Matt 9:14-17) for the next Matthaean account is of a controversy about fasting, since the disciples of Jesus did not conform to the practice either of the Pharisees or of the disciples of the Baptist. Controversy over fasting customs lasted into the period of the church (cf. Didache 8; Epistle of Barnabas 3); to the evangelist the matter is one which concerns the freedom of Christians from earlier traditions. To this pericope Luke adds "And no man having drunk of old desireth new; for he saith, The old is good." This would seem to be a tradition handed down independently, which Luke has added because of its reference to wine. It may represent an argument he has met in his own ministry.

Luke 6:1-11. The Sabbath. So far Luke has been able in this part of the Gospel to follow Matthew's order, but there are two other narratives in Matthew (12:1-14) which treat the same subject, the controversies aroused by the actions of Jesus and the justification of his behavior. Luke therefore brings them in at this point. Like the earlier stories, they deal with issues that were still of importance in the life of the early church. Both are concerned with the keeping of the sabbath, the one because of the actions of the disciples of Jesus plucking ears of corn and the other from the cure of a man with a withered hand. Matthew introduces the first as "at that time" (12:1) and the second by saying "and he departed thence, and went into their synagogue" (12:9). As Luke has taken them out of their Matthaean context, he simply begins the first with "on a sabbath" and the second with "on another sabbath." The first leads to a declaration that "the Son of man is Lord of the sabbath"; the second makes the challenge that it is lawful to do good on the sabbath. It is noticeable that Luke includes the reference to David (6:2), which would be understood by those familiar with the Old Testament, but omits Matthew's reference to what the Law permitted the priests in the temple, which would be less interesting to his readers.

Luke's text for the healing of the withered hand differs in some way from Matthew's and is perhaps modified by his having a different version also at his disposal. The story is of a pair with the healing of the man with the dropsy, recorded by Luke alone (14:1-6), and Matthew has perhaps added words from a version of this at Matt 22:11-12.

Luke 6:13-49. The Great Sermon. Luke has now been able to give a picture of Jesus' Minstry and to speak of the opposition Jesus encountered during its course. Having set this scene, Luke can now begin to speak of Christ's teaching to his disciples, with the Twelve as the chosen band to carry on his work. He can now in effect fill up the gap he left by passing over the Sermon on the Mount. At the beginning of the sermon, Matthew had said that "his disciples came" to Jesus, and later gives their names in parentheses ("Now the names of the twelve apostles are these," Matt 10:2-4) when speaking of their being sent out on a mission. The "disciples" covers a wider number than the Twelve, but it was clearly convenient for Luke to name the Twelve here: "And when it was day, he called his disciples, and he chose from them twelve, whom he also called apostles" (6:13). Luke also adds a summary note that there was "a great multitude of his disciples, and a great number of people from all Judæa and Jerusalem, and the sea coast of Tyre and Sidon" (6:17).

It is misleading to distinguish Matthew's and Luke's versions of the great sermon as being the one "on the mount" and the other "on the plain." Both speak of Jesus going "to the mount" (εἰς τὸ ὄρος), though this is sometimes obscured by translating, as for instance in the first edition of RSV, the phrase in Matthew as "on the mountain" (5:1) and in Luke as "into the hills" (6:12).[11] No doubt we are meant by both to think of the hill country rather than of a mountain as we usually think of one, and when Luke says that Jesus came down and "stood on a level place" (6:17) he is only adding a detail to Matthew's picture.

The differences between the two forms are obvious, from the variations in the Beatitudes onwards. That Luke shows some dependence on Matthew for the form of the sermon would appear to be illustrated by his words "But I say unto you" (Luke 6:27; Matt 5:44) when he has not included the earlier words of Matthew "Ye have heard it said," and by the words that follow the sermon: "After he had ended all his sayings" (Luke 7:1) corresponding to Matthew's "And it came to pass when Jesus had finished these words" (Matt 7:28); and by the story of the centurion's servant following in sequence (Luke having already used the story of the leper). There are however two great differences between the two forms of the sermon: (1) that Luke omits all that specifically applies to the concern of Christian living in a predominantly Jewish environment, with reference to such things as the righteousness of the scribes and Pharisees or to Jewish customs about almsgiving, prayer, and fasting; and (2) that a good deal of Jesus'

---

[11]This was corrected in second edition RSV to read "to the mountain."

teaching included in Matthew's text is left over by Luke for the next part of the Gospel—"all that Jesus began to teach."

The case for the dependence of Luke on Matthew does not depend on a particular conclusion as to whether the text of our canonical Matthew is in some ways a revision of an earlier form, and still less on the supposition that we can know the exact form Luke would have before him. But it is noticeable that Matthew's sermon does show signs of a secondary editorial hand. It becomes a more shapely composition if some of its contents are omitted. Lagrange for instance comments, "When one seeks to establish the sequence of ideas in Matthew, one perceives that some passages have the appearance of additions." Lagrange lists seven such passages: Matt 5:13-16, 24-26; 6:7-15, 19-34; 7:7-11, 22-23, and adds that none of these passages is found in Luke's version "although they are found elsewhere, often in a better context. This confirmation of internal criticism by the authority of another evangelist is of the most satisfying kind."[12]

There is however another remarkable fact. There is a great difference of the degree of identity between Matthew's text and Luke's in the passages Luke has in his sermon and those he includes elsewhere. The degree of identity is much greater in the latter group. One might have expected the opposite. The most probable solution of the question seems to be that Luke followed both his sources, Proto-Matthew and another, closely, and that the text of Proto-Matthew has been modified by the editor who later extended it. Luke's form of the Beatitudes (Luke 6:20b-26) would for instance seem to have been taken from Proto-Matthew.

Luke 7:1-10. The Centurion's Servant. Having already included the healing of a leper (5:12-16) Luke continues with the next narrative in Matthew's sequence, the healing of a centurion's servant. Like Matthew, Luke begins by saying that Jesus entered Capernaum, but before keeping close to Matthew's text he inserts additional material from a different tradition of the incident, relating the intercession of "elders of the Jews" on the centurion's behalf.

In speaking of the sick person, Mathew refers to him by the word παῖς which might mean either "child" or "servant"; Luke avoids the difficulty by using the word δοῦλος, "servant" in his narrative, but at 7:6 when spoken words form the bulk of the text, Luke begins to follow Matthew's words very closely, and significantly keeps παῖς where Matthew has it. At the close of the story Matthew (8:11-12) inserts a general statement which looks like an insertion into his own account: "Many shall come from the east and the west"; Luke either

---

[12]Marie Joseph Lagrange, *Évangile selon saint Matthieu*, Études bibliques, 7th ed. (Paris: J. Gabalda, 1948; ¹1923) 78. Of the seven examples Lagrange gives six are wholly and the seventh partly included in the list of additions made to the text of Proto-Matthew in the tentative reconstruction of Proto-Matthew in my *The First Gospel* (Macon GA: Mercer University Press, 1992) 121-24.

omits it, or else did not find it here in his copy of Matthew; he uses the same material later on.

Luke 7:11–8:3. The Signs of the Messiah. In dealing with "all that Jesus began to do" Luke has therefore covered all the material of the First Gospel as far as Matt 8:17. Passing over the intermediate material, he resumes his use of it at Matt 11:2. At first sight this may look as a desertion of Matthew's order, but the matter calls for closer scrutiny. The material omitted here consists of the following sections.

(a) Matt 8:18-22. Two Claimants to Discipleship.
(b) Matt 8:23-27. Stilling the Storm.
(c) Matt 8:28-34. The Gadarene Demoniacs.
(d) Matt 9:1-17. Stories of Controversies.
(e) Matt 9:18-26. Jairus's Daughter and the Woman with the Issue of Blood.
(f) Matt 9:27-34. Healings of the Blind and Dumb.
(g) Matt 9:35–11:1. The Discourse on Discipleship.

Of these seven groups of material that of the Stories of Controversies (d) has already been used by Luke; that of the Healings of the Blind and Dumb (f), doublets of material found elsewhere in Matthew (20:29-34 and 12:22-24) are additions to Proto-Matthew which would not have been in Luke's copy; and (g) is the kind of material he needs for the next main part of the Gospel ("all that Jesus began to teach") and the story of Claimants to Discipleship (a) is left over to provide an introduction to that theme. This leaves the three narratives of the Stilling of the Storm (b), the Gadarene Demoniacs (c), and Jairus's Daughter and the Woman with the Issue of Blood (d) which Luke will use later in the same relative sequence. Apart from the one interruption caused by this transference, Luke is to follow Matthew's own order of events without break until the end of the first half of his Gospel (Luke 9:50).

The omission of the material of Matt 8:18–11:1 at this point enables Luke to come to the question of the Baptist from his prison: "Art thou he that cometh?" For Luke there is no more appropriate continuation for his narrative: he has opened his account of Jesus' Ministry with the proclamation "The Spirit of the Lord is upon me, because he anointed me to preach good tidings to the poor; he hath sent me to proclaim release to the captives," and Matthew's text gives him the corresponding reply of Jesus to John: "Go your way, and tell John what things ye have seen and heard; the blind receive their sight, the lame walk, the lepers are cleansed, and the deaf hear, the dead are raised up, the poor have good tidings preached to them" (Luke 7:22; Matt 11:4-5). Luke has now spoken of Jesus' miracles, and, as in the Great Sermon, the good news has been preached. The episode of John's questioning provides an appropriate and timely comment.

The actual words of the reply to John include some claims that have not been specifically illustrated in Luke's Gospel. He has not mentioned any deaf or blind person being healed nor any dead person being raised. Partly to cover this, Luke adds to his narrative "on many that were blind he bestowed sight" (7:21) but can hardly speak so incidentally of the dead being raised. In Matthew there is no problem: the daughter of Jairus has already been mentioned. Luke therefore inserts an account of his own dealing with John's question: he records the raising of the widow's son at Nain (Luke 7:11-17). For Luke the story (the Palestinian origin of which is shown by the reference to such an obscure village) has the added interest which comes from his evident concern about widows. Luke has mentioned the widow Anna in the temple, a widow is a character in one of his parables (18:3), a poor widow gives her all in the temple treasury (21:2), and there are other references in Acts (6:1; 9:39, 41). Concern for widows was of importance in the life of the early church (cf. 1 Tim 5:3ff.).

So Luke passes to the questioning of John, and the witness of Jesus to John, as in Matthew, keeping very close to Matthew's text. Both John and Jesus had met with opposition, though the criticisms made about them were different. Jesus was criticized for not being an ascetic like John; for being "a friend of publicans and sinners" (Luke 7:34).

The whole group of episodes is then rounded off by a Lucan summary (8:1-3): Jesus continued his preaching in the company of the Twelve, and with women who ministered to his needs. The women are later to be mentioned again (23:55 and 24:10). When they reappear, Mary Magdalene and Joanna are mentioned without description, as they are here introduced more fully: "Mary that was called Magdalene, from whom seven devils had gone out, and Joanna the wife of Chuza, Herod's steward."

<u>Luke 8:4-21. The Parable of the Sower.</u> Omitting the controversies about evil spirits and signs (Matt 12:25-45) to be dealt with in the second part of the Gospel in the exposition of Christ's teaching, Luke comes to the collection of parables that forms the third of the great Matthaean discourses. As in dealing with the Sermon on the Mount, Luke recognized its place as a necessary element in describing Christ's ministry, but is noticeably shorter than Matthew both in the parable and in its interpretation. One of the pairs of parables also found in Matthew, the Mustard Seed and the Leaven, has its parallel elsewhere in Luke; it appears to be an addition to Proto-Matthew, absent from the text available to Luke. Luke transfers Matthew's introduction to this section (13:46-50) to the end, modifying the words "Whosoever shall do the will of my Father which is in heaven, he is my brother, and sister, and mother" to read "My mother and my brethren are those which hear the word of God and do it" (Luke 8:21), applying them more closely to the meaning of the parable and providing a "climax."

Two details with regard to the parable may be noted. Matthew has given it a precise setting in time and place: "On that day went Jesus out of the house, and sat by the sea side" (Matt 13:1); Luke, having transferred the narrative to a different position, simply says: "And when a great multitude came together" (8:4). And in the interpretation following Luke adds a group of three sayings (8:16-19), each of which has a parallel elsewhere in Luke (11:33; 12:2; 19:26), and also in different places in Matthew (5:15; 10:16; 25:29). Both Luke and the editor of

Matthew have fitted in sayings which have been preserved in different contexts. The third of them (Luke 8:18) is paralleled also in Matt 13:12 in connection with the parable of the Sower, but each of them has a parallel elsewhere in Luke (11:33; 12:2; 19:26) and also in Matthew (5:15; 10:16; 25:29). They are sayings which have been preserved in different contexts, and both Luke and the editor of Matthew have been careful to preserve them. There are of course minor differences between the various traditions, as when Matt 5:15 and Luke 11:33 speak of a light being put "under a bushel" and Luke 8:16 has "under a bed."[13]

Luke 8:22-56. Three Miracles. Luke now sets about filling in the episodes he has left over from Matt 8:23 onwards. The first of these is that of the Stilling of the Storm (8:22-25; Matt 8:18, 23-27). As before, having altered Matthew's order, Luke avoids giving a precise context as in Matt 8:18 and simply says, "Now it came to pass on one of those days." As in Matthew, the story is linked with that of the demoniac "in the country of the Gerasenes, which is over against Galilee" (a characteristic word of explanation). For the details Luke is clearly not wholly dependent on Matthew, who calls the country that of the "Gadarenes" and who speaks of two demoniacs; nor has Matthew all the details of Luke's version.

Matthew then records Jesus' return across the lake (9:1) and Luke includes a similar connecting note (8:40). Matthew has however already used the material that follows as far as 9:18, where he comes to the raising of Jairus's daughter, with the account of the healing of the woman with a hemorrhage. Again Luke has a fuller account, particularly in the included story, but his order is strictly the same as Matthew's.

Luke 9:1-9. Sending Out the Twelve. Without the short narratives of healing (Matt 9:27-34), doublets which probably were not in Matthew's original text, Luke continues in Matthew's sequence with the sending out of the Twelve; but whereas for Matthew this is the beginning of the second of his long discourses (Matt 9:15–10:39), Luke, who reserves such material for the later part of his Gospel, confines himself to the actual sending forth. He has no need to include the list of the names of the Twelve (Matt 10:2-4), which he has already given; and he omits the introduction "Go not into any way of the Gentiles, and enter not into any city of the Samaritans" (Matt 10:5), which no longer corresponds to the situation of the Christian mission by the time he was writing. Luke treats Matthew's discourses as he has done the Sermon on the Mount and the collection of parables: he takes account of it as showing what Jesus has been doing, but still leaves over the exposition of Jesus' teaching.

Luke can now skip a long section of Matthew, which (with the same reservation) he has already used. This brings him to the note in Matt 14:1-2 concerning Herod's opinion of Christ. To Matthew, this is a useful introduction to the account of the Baptist's death, but that is irrelevant to Luke's main theme,

---

[13]Mark, as often, conflates Matthew's and Luke's wording, and has "under a bushel, or under a bed" (Mark 4:21). Cf. Mark 1:32, conflated from Matt 8:16 and Luke 4:40.

from which he does not allow himself to be distracted, and it is therefore omitted. The reference to Herod does however serve as conveniently pointing to the part Herod is to play in the Passion narrative (Luke 23:6-12). Luke therefore extends Matthew's note, to include the words of Herod and their consequences: "Who is this, about whom I hear such things? And he sought to see him." Luke alone of the evangelists tells us that in the end he was to see him.

As, unlike Matthew and Mark, Luke does not relate the story of the Baptist's death, he adds an editorial note (9:10) of the return of the Twelve from their mission, and passes on to Matthew's next narrative, the Feeding of the Five Thousand.

Luke 9:10-17. The Feeding of the Five Thousand. The multiplication of the loaves is recorded in two forms in Matthew and Mark (the Feeding of the Five Thousand and of the Four Thousand), and once in Luke and John. A comparison of the six accounts shows clearly that the story was widely circulated in the Christian communities, and that none of the evangelists was entirely dependent on any other. The narrative is in effect part of a sequence of themes, not all of which are included by Luke: the feeding of the multitude; Jesus' retirement to the hills; the crossing of the lake; the demand for a sign; and Peter's confession. In view of this, as well as from their internal correspondence, it seems clear that the two accounts in Matthew and Mark are variant forms of the same tradition. Of all the four evangelists John seems to show the greatest knowledge of the topography of the lake (which he calls "of Tiberias" as well as "of Galilee") and Mark the least. Of all the accounts, that in John shows the signs of being the most "primitive," as it is also the most circumstantial.[14]

John begins by saying that Jesus went across the sea, and this is entirely consistent with the statement in Matthew and Mark that he went to a "desert place" (that is, a lonely place), by boat in the story of the Five Thousand (Matt 14:13; 15:33; Mark 6:32; 8:4). Luke also so describes the place (9:12), though he begins by saying that Jesus "withdrew apart to a city called Bethsaida." In view of Luke's own account this can only mean that the scene was in the country near Bethsaida, which will presumably be included among the "villages" of Matt 14:15 and Mark 6:33. Luke's reference to Bethsaida is therefore consistent with the other accounts; that he is more specific is an indication that he is not wholly dependent on Matthew or Mark. All six accounts then relate the feeding of the multitude; John has an added detail in the reference to Philip and Andrew (6:7-8), and both John and Mark, independently of each other, to the "two hundred denarii" (Mark 6:37; John 6:7), a clear indication of widespread knowledge of the story.

---

[14]Cf. John A. T. Robinson, *Redating the New Testament* (London: SCM Press; Philadelphia: Westminster Press, 1976) 302n.254.

After the feeding, both accounts in Matthew and Mark (Matt 14:22; 15:39; Mark 6:45; 8:10) speak of crossing the sea; the earlier account makes Jesus himself take first to the hills, and John has the added and significant note that it was because "they were about to come and take him by force, to make him king" (6:15). In Matt 14 the boat crosses over to Gennesaret (v. 34); Mark, who is following Matthew and was presumably confused by not knowing the site of Bethsaida with which Luke shows that the story was already connected, makes the boat set out for Bethsaida, but with Matthew says it arrived at Gennesaret.

The reference to Gennesaret is consistent with the statement in John that the crowd moved on to Capernaum and found Jesus "on the other side of the sea"; what is less clear is what is meant to be the end of the journey after the accounts of the Four Thousand. According to Matthew, Jesus "came into the borders of Magadan"; if this means Magdala, it could still be a true reminiscence, and would still fit in with Jesus ending up at Capernaum. Mark has "the parts of the Dalmanutha," and it is impossible to know what is meant by this, if indeed it is what he actually wrote. Following Matthew, Mark records the demand for a sign (Matt 16:1-4; Mark 8:11-13), with which may be compared John 6:30; afterwards Mark, whose first journey set out for Bethsaida, at last brings Jesus there (8:22) and records the healing of a blind man.

The series of narratives ends with the confesion of Peter, which in John follows on the Feeding of the Five Thousand, apparently after an interval from the speech at Capernaum when "many disciples" no longer "walked with" Jesus. In John Jesus was confessed as "the Holy One of God" (John 6:69). For Matthew and Mark the confession of Jesus as the Christ (Mark) or "the Christ, the son of the living God" (Matthew) follows the second account of feeding. Luke also has the confession of "the Christ of God," but before it he has omitted the crossing of the sea, and all that follows in Matthew (and Mark) to this point.

For those who have accepted Marcan priority, this has been the "great omission" by Luke of Mark 6:45–8:26. Streeter felt compelled to "ask whether Luke's 'great omission' can be explained by any other hypothesis than the absence of the material from his source,"[15] and tentatively suggested that Luke used a mutilated copy of Mark. If however it was Matthew, not Mark, that Luke was using, the difficulty disappears. Two of Mark's pericopes (the healing of the deaf mute, 7:32-37, and of a blind man, 8:22-26) are not in Matthew. Luke moreover has not unlimited space, and moves rapidly from the Feeding of the Five Thousand to Peter's Confession (a connection which would seem to have had support in common tradition) and to the Transfiguration to complete the first half of his Gospel. To do this, Luke omits the walking on the sea (Matt 14:22-33) and inevitably therefore the healings that followed (Matt 14:34-36). Luke was

---

[15]B. H. Streeter, *The Four Gospels. A Study of Origins, Treating of the Manuscript Tradition, Sources, Authorship, and Dates* (London: Macmillan, 1924; New York: St. Martin's Press, 1956) 175.

certain to omit the passage about the Tradition of the Elders, which was irrelevant for his purpose, and could also omit the further healings after that; the account of the plea of the woman of Canaan might in any case have been an embarrassment for Luke's Gentile readers. The second account of feeding the thousands, if it was indeed in Luke's copy of Matthew, was clearly unnecessary to Luke for him to develop his Gospel; but that narrative, like that of the attempt of Peter to walk on the water (Matt 14:28-33) and the Commission to Peter (Matt 16:17-29) were probably later additions to Proto-Matthew. Luke's omissions may not have been very great, and are wholly understandable.

Luke 9:18-27. Peter's Confession. The confession of Jesus as the Christ is an element of the Gospel that Luke cannot omit. Matthew records it as taking place at Caesarea Philippi, but Luke ignores this. All he is concerned with is that in response to Jesus' question to the disciples, "Who do you say that I am?" Peter makes the great confession, "The Christ of God." This is what all that has happened has taught the disciples, and what the readers have been led to believe. So, without Matthew's narrative both of the promise to Peter and of the subsequent rebuke to him, Luke concludes the section with Jesus' prediction of the death and resurrection that are the lot of the Christ. In Jesus' words it is "the Son of man" who is to suffer; it is only after the Resurrection that Luke puts this in the form that "the Christ" must suffer. Jesus had said "while he was still in Galilee that the Son of man must be delivered into the hands of sinful men" (Luke 24:6-7); after the Resurrection it could be seen that it was necessary "that the Christ should suffer" (24:26, 46). Luke is careful to keep to Jesus' own words. That Christians must share in suffering like their Lord (Luke 9:22-27) is a further corollary of their following Jesus. The point is heightened in Luke by the addition of "daily" to the Matthaean words about taking up the cross.

Luke 9:28-50. The Transfiguration and After. So Luke comes to the Transfiguration, the great climax of his account of "all that Jesus began to do." Like Matthew, Luke ends with "Jesus alone" after the voice from the cloud has proclaimed "This is my Son, my Chosen [or my Beloved]: hear ye him" (9:35). This is the second of the three great peaks of Christ's manifestation, after which the command "hear ye him" will be met by an exposition of Christ's teaching.

Luke's account of the Transfiguration is not entirely dependent on Matthew, and he adds that Moses and Elijah were talking with Jesus about his departure (ἔξοδος) which he was to accomplish at Jerusalem. So far the Gospel has been concerned with the coming of Jesus, to which Luke refers in Acts 13:24 in an unusual phrase: "when John had first preached before his coming [lit. before the face of his coming] the baptism of repentance." The word used there for "coming" is εἴσοδος, the correlative of ἔξοδος. Now the rest of Luke, from 9:51 onwards, will also be looking forward to the "Exodus" of Jesus, through death and resurrection to ascension, "the days of his being received up."

Luke now comes quickly to the end of the first half of the Gospel. He omits Matt 17:9-13, with the disciples' question about the coming of Elijah, simply

taking from it the note that the disciples were silent in those days about what
they had seen. From the rest of Matthew's narrative Luke includes the healing
of the epileptic boy, as following on the Transfiguration, and the second
prediction of the Passion, adding to Matthew the words "Let these things sink
into your ears" to reinforce the words of the first prediction. Matthew's story of
the temple tax (Matt 17:24-27) is no longer relevant to Luke's readers and is
omitted. But Luke includes Matthew's words about the dispute as to who was the
greatest (characteristically omitting "at that hour" since he has broken Matthew's
context), and adds to Matthew's text the warning of Jesus to his disciples: "He
that is not against you is for you" (Luke 9:37-50).

"All that Jesus began to teach"

At 9:51 Luke begins the next main division of his Gospel, in which he sets
out more fully the teaching of Jesus: "And it came to pass, when the days were
being fulfilled that he should be received up, he set his face to go to Jerusalem."
The setting is that of a gradual approach to Jerusalem, with periodic reminders
of this (9:51; 10:38; 13:22; 17:11; 18:31), but they are of a very general nature
until the approach to Jericho at the end of the journey (18:35).[16] Before that only
two references are to a particular locality: a village of the Samaritans (9:52) and
"between Samaria and Galilee" (17:11). In both cases the reference is necessary
for the point of the story: in the first because of the objection that "his face was
set towards Jerusalem," arousing Samaritan prejudices, in the second because the
ten lepers there included a Samaritan. For Luke makes no attempt to plot a
journey: he is reminding his readers of where the work of Jesus was leading him
and putting the record of Jesus' teaching in this setting because he has now
abandoned the order of incidents in Matthew. That will only matter again when
the narrative deals with the events in Jerusalem.

It would therefore be misleading to suppose that from 9:51 onwards Luke
is professing to give an account of a final journey, chronologically later than the
events previously reported. From the time of the Temptation Jesus had been
travelling about: he moved about Galilee where "he taught in their synagogues"
(4:15); he was "preaching in the synagogues of Judaea" (4:44, "Judaea" in the
sense of "of the Jews" geographically including Galilee); "he went about through
cities and villages, preaching and bringing the gospel of the kingdom of God"
(8:1). The words of Luke 13:34 indeed imply other visits to Jerusalem, as Jesus
said "How often would I have gathered thy children together, even as a hen
gathereth her own brood under her wings, and ye would not!" It is after the first

---

[16]Cf. C. H. Dodd's note in *Historical Tradition in the Fourth Gospel* (Cambridge:
Cambridge University Press, 1963) 63: "In Luke 9:57 πορευομένων αὐτῶν ἐν τῇ ὁδῷ
means 'once when they were on a journey,' Luke 17:12 εἰσερχομένου αὐτοῦ εἴς τινα
κώμην 'once as he was entering a village' (cf. Luke 11:29; Matt 17:24; etc.)."

prediction of the Passion (9:22), followed by the Transfiguration and the reference to the Exodus "which he was to accomplish at Jerusalem" (9:31), and the second prediction of the Passion, that the end of the wandering must be kept in view. It is also the more relevant that to speak of Jerusalem as the goal comes in at this point (9:51) in that Jesus was being rejected at a village of the Samaritans for that very reason. So it was "as they went in the way" (9:57) that we are told of would-be disciples: Jesus "having put his hand to the plough" was not looking back (9:62). Again at Luke 10:32 it is still pointed out that "they went on their way" and at 13:22 that Jesus "went on his way through cities and villages, teaching, and journeying on unto Jerusalem."

These words are indeed a fair description of this part of the Gospel. The reader is to learn from Jesus' teaching, but not to forget that in his teaching he was always on the way to a goal, to Jerusalem and the Passion. Some of the teaching included was given in Galilee, and the context may reveal this, as in 13:31 where Jesus was in Herod's territory, but the reminder is still given, it would be Jerusalem that would see his death (13:32ff.). It is when that goal was, as it were, actually in sight that we are brought back to geography, with the words of Jesus "Behold, we go up to Jerusalem" (18:31), with a repeated warning of the Passion which is now imminent. After that we do have place names: Jesus is at Jericho (18:35); then "nigh to Jerusalem" (19:11); then "nigh unto Bethphage and Bethany" (19:29); and so to the city itself.

That the order of Luke's material from 9:51 up to 18:15 (the point at which Luke resumes Matthew's order) does not depend on topography is clear enough from the way he has collected together groups of teaching, much of it found in earlier contexts in Matthew. It is to the teaching itself that we have to look to see what order there actually is.

A systematic attempt to provide a solution was made by C. F. Evans in his essay "The Central Section of St Luke's Gospel."[17] "Commentators," he says, "have been at a loss what to make of it."[18] He asks whether it is not possible that Luke "has selected and ordered his material with a view to presenting it as a Christian Deuteronomy,"[19] and in support of this thesis sets out an analysis of Deuteronomy 1–26 in twenty-two sections, with sections of Luke 9:51–18:14 set alongside. Evans admits that "some of the resemblances of subject matter and wording in these parallels may be fortuitous," but urges that "what is more strik- ing . . . as generally in questions of this kind, is the correspondence of order," and that "the conclusion is difficult to resist that the evangelist has selected and

---

[17]In *Studies in the Gospels: Essays in Memory of R. H. Lightfoot*, ed. Dennis E. Nineham (Oxford: Blackwell, 1955).

[18]Ibid., 40.

[19]Ibid., 42.

arranged his material in such a way as to present it in a Deuteronomistic sequence."[20]

At first sight this is a very attractive hypothesis, but it does not bear too close an examination. Evans cites parallels, either of subject matter or of wording. Many of the connections are obscure, and depend on slight verbal resemblances, and it is difficult to imagine Luke going systematically through Deuteronomy and his Gospel sources in order to make them. For example, Deut 14:18, dealing with tithing, and Luke 13:6-9 are put in parallel on the ground that Deuteronomy speaks of tithes "every third year" (LXX μετὰ τρία ἔτη) and Luke speaks of the unfruitful fig tree: "Lo, these three years have I come seeking fruit" (τρία ἔτη ἀφ' οὖ ἔρχομαι ζητῶν καρπόν). The only resemblance seems to be the reference to three years.

The scheme as put forward by Evans seems to get off to a very good start in his first three sections, which look more convincing parallels than some of his later ones. The three sections therefore deserve a closer look. They are as follows.

(1) Deut 1. Israel goes with Moses from the mountain of Horeb. Twelve men are sent to search out the land, and return with fruit from it.
Luke 10:1-3, 17-20. The disciples go with Jesus from the mountain of the Transfiguration. Seventy are sent out. The harvest is plentiful, and the Seventy return with good news. "Into every town and place where he himself was about to come" is cited as a parallel with Deut 1:22.

(2) Deut 2:1–3.22. Moses sent messengers to Sihon and Og, with a message of peace, for food and drink. They were rejected, and the cities were destroyed.
Luke 10:4-16. Jesus sent out the Seventy, to eat and drink whatever was offered them. Cities like Chorazin would be destroyed because of their rejection of the Lord. "The Lord" is the only verbal parallel cited.

(3) Deut 3:23–4:40. At that season Moses prays to the God of heaven and earth. He urges the people to keep their wisdom and understanding. They have heard the voice of God and have seen his fire.
Luke 10:21-24. At that hour Jesus thanks the Father, Lord of heaven and earth; things hidden from the wise and understanding are revealed to babes. The disciples are blessed for what they have seen and heard. "At that hour" (ἐν αὐτῇ ὥρᾳ) and "wise and understanding" (σοφῶ καὶ συνετῶ) are cited as parallels.

In making this precis of Evans's text I have sought to bring out all his points. Put this way they look convincing. They are less obvious in the actual text of Scripture where the passage from Deuteronomy (1:1–4:40) is about six times as long as that in Luke; and incidentally Evans has rearranged Luke's order (as 10:1-3, 17-20, and 10:4-16). So far as verbal reminiscence is concerned, it is

---

[20]Ibid., 50.

not surprising that Luke uses Old Testament phrases, either from this or some other part of Deuteronomy, or indeed from any other book. What is more significant is the matter of order ("as generally in questions of this kind," to recall Evans's words), and what is certain is that the order of these three sections is not copied by Luke from Deuteronomy, for it is the order of the same material in Matthew, although not in one continuous narrative (Matt 9:35-38; 10:9-16; 11:20-27; 13:16-17). The material in Matthew is interspersed with items Luke has already used, and with some teaching on other subjects he has still to treat of, but it is Matthew's order that controls Luke's own. Moreover, the three sections are preceded by 9:57-60, which are parallel to Matt 8:19-22, that is, in the same sequence, with material already accounted for by Luke interspersed immediately before.

Luke's section on the Apostolic Commission is a compact unit, and the use he has made of Matthew in its construction can be seen in the following table, with the sections of Luke shown parallel with the corresponding material in Matthew and his omissions in a separate column.

LUKE	MATTHEW	MATTHEW, omitted by Luke
9:57-62	8:18-22	
		8:23–9:26, already used by Luke.
		9:27-34, two doublets (cf. Matt 20:29-34; 12:22-24) not in Proto-Matthew as I have argued in *The First Gospel*
10:1-12	9:35–10:16	
		10:17-42, on conditions of discipleship, also additions to Proto-Matthew; Luke has a parallel later
10:13-22	11:20-30	
		12:1-21, already used by Luke.
		12:22-45, on demand for signs and casting out demons, left over by Luke for separate treatment later
10:23-24	13:16-17	

If Luke has Matthew at his disposal it is clear there is no need to turn to Deuteronomy for an explanation of his order; his procedure is both simple and direct.

So far as parallels with Deuteronomy within each of these sections are concerned, it is to be observed that in the first of them Matthew would have provided a better parallel than Luke. It was *twelve* men that Moses sent, and Matthew's charge to the apostles is to the Twelve, not the Seventy. In the second, a much closer parallel to Luke could have been found in Deut 20:10-15 ("Proclaim peace unto it. And it shall be, if it make thee answer of peace. . . . And if it will make no peace with thee . . . "—with the destruction of the hostile cities). In the third section Evans cites ἐν αὐτῇ τῇ ὥρᾳ in Luke as parallel with Deuteronomy ἐν τῷ καιρῷ ἐκείνῳ; Matthew has the much closer ἐν ἐκείνῳ τῷ καιρῷ; and the other verbal parallels are common to Matthew and Luke.

It would be tedious to pursue this through the whole of Evans's list. The point should already be clear that it is not to Deuteronomy but to Matthew that we must turn to get any clue to Luke's order. The earlier part of the Gospel has already shown what value Luke attached to Matthew; we see the same thing here. Luke however is setting out Jesus' teaching on a different plan from that of Matthew's great discourses, and also adding much new material. It is by following him stage by stage that we can enter into the development of Luke's thought.

Luke 9:51–10:24. The Apostolic Commission. The first of Matthew's five blocks of teaching material is the Sermon on the Mount. Luke has already drawn upon some of this; some also falls outside the special interests of Luke's non-Palestinian readers; and the rest deals with a variety of different subjects. It is therefore natural that Luke should start this part of his own Gospel with the subject of Matthew's second discourse, the commission to the apostles. It is indeed in line with his own description of his Gospel: "All that Jesus began to do and to teach, until the day in which he was received up, after he had given commandment through the Holy Spirit unto the apostles whom he had chosen" (Acts 1:1-2). To this commission Luke prefaces the incidents of the refusal of would-be disciples (called by Matthew "a scribe" and "another of his disciples" but by Luke merely "someone" and "another," with "another" not mentioned in Matthew's text). Luke and the editor of Matthew seem to have drawn this from a common source; the insertion into Matthew has been made less neatly than that into Luke.

In following Matthew's order of events, Luke has already mentioned the commissioning of the Twelve, and therefore, while covering Matthew's material, he now gives the instrucitons for the apostles as addressed to the seventy (or seventy-two) about whom he must have learned from a different tradition. This is not only clear from Luke's reference to the seventy, but also from the fact that his text is not a closely, but a lightly edited version of Matthew's. Allowing for this, we can easily follow his use of Matthew. Omitting the material from which he has already taken all he needs, Luke comes to Matt 9:35–10:16, the commission to the apostles. As he is using a tradition with regard to the seventy, Luke omits the names of the Twelve, which he has already given. At Matt 10:17 the theme of the discourse in the First Gospel changes from the Apostolate on to the persecution of Christians, and this appears to be an addition to Proto-Matthew which would not be in Luke's copy. Then follows the passage about the witness of John: Luke passes over this and resumes at Matt 11:20 with the Woes on the Unbelieving Cities. Closing his account of the Seventy by recording their return (10:17-20), Luke adds Christ's Thanksgiving to the Father and the blessedness of his disciples, which has a parallel in Matt 13:16-17. The account of the return of the seventy must go back to Luke's special source for the commission to them; the rest of the material after the commission (that is, Luke 10:13-16, 21-

23) is not only in Matthew's sequence but is also a close copy of Matthew's wording.

Luke 10:25-42. Love of God and Neighbor. From the subject of the apostolic commission Luke proceeds to that of the love of God and of our neighbor, turning for a while from copying Matthew to material from some other source or sources. It begins, in a form different from that of Matthew, with the lawyer's question, "What shall I do to inherit eternal life?" (10:25-28). The difference both in form and content points to Luke's independence of Matthew, though he incidentally covers the material of Matt 22:34-40. The episode leads into the parable of the Good Samaritan (10:29-37), with its final words "Go and do thou likewise."

Like that parable, the story of Martha and Mary that follows is a sort of counterpoint to Luke 9:51-56. Then it was that a village would not receive Jesus; now the village of Martha and Mary welcomes him. The churlishness of the Samaritans in one village has been counterbalanced in the story of the Good Samaritan.

The little episode of Martha and Mary is one of the indications of traditions common to Luke and the Fourth Gospel. Presumably Luke did not know that, as John relates, they lived at Bethany. To Luke they are simply in "a certain village." The story is told merely for its lesson, but its presence in Luke is an unintentional witness to the existence of traditions that Jesus' ministry was not confined to Galilee. "The characters of the two sisters as represented in John are true to the picture in the present story."[21]

Luke 11:1-13. On Prayer. There follows a new subject, prayer. It begins with the formal opening "And it came to pass, that as he was praying in a certain place," both the time and the place being left deliberately vague, and passes on to the giving of the Lord's Prayer (11:1-4). Both the setting and the form of the prayer are different from Matthew's, and it is probable that Luke quotes the prayer in the form with which he was familiar in the churches he knew best. The reference to John is an indication that Luke was drawing on a different tradition from that represented in Matthew; it is not likely he invented it. The teaching on prayer is then illustrated by the parable of the Friend at Midnight (11:5-8), after which Luke reinforces the lesson by a quotation which has a parallel inserted into Matthew's Sermon on the Mount (Matt 7:7-11; Luke 11:9-13).

Luke 11:14-54. Openness to the Truth. Still leaving aside for further inclusion what Matthew (10:16-25) records about the coming persecution of Christian disciples, Luke then deals with all the material he has not already used, up to the point where Matthew's collection of parables began (Matt 13:1). Immediately before his discourse on the apostolic commission Matthew had quoted the accusation of the Pharisees made against Jesus: "By the prince of the

---

[21]J. M. Creed, *The Gospel according to St Luke* (London, 1930) in loc.

demons casteth he out demons" (9:34). At the close of the discourse, he refers
to this again: "If they have called the master of the house Beelzebul" (10:25). It
is the subject of the first section of Matthew's Gospel for Luke to come to, as
he passes over what he has already dealt with, and finds himself at Matt 12:22,
the natural subject therefore for him to deal with next.

Matthew deals with three matters in this order: (1) the Beelzebul controversy, 12:22-37; (2) the demand for signs, 12:38-42; and (3) the return of the evil
spirit, 12:43-45. Luke very understandably changes the order to deal with
questions of Beelzebul and evil spirits together and to put the demand for signs
last. But he still brackets the subjects together by prefacing the words "But some
of them said, By Beelzebul the prince of the demons casteth he out demons. And
others tempting him, sought of him a sign from heaven" (11:15-16).

Luke therefore relates the story of the controversy about Beelzebul and the
words about the return of the evil spirit. At this point in Matthew (12:46-50)
there is added the incident of the coming of Jesus' mother and brothers, with the
saying "Whosoever shall do the will of my Father which is in heaven, he is my
brother, and sister, and mother." Luke has already used this pericope (8:19-21)
with the variant wording "those who hear the word of God and keep it." Instead
of repeating this, therefore, he now replaces it with another incident also connected with Jesus' mother (11:27-28) which has the same lesson: "Rather blessed
are they that hear the word of God and keep it." It is an interesting example of
Luke's reflecting Matthew's order, even when using different material.

So Luke passes to what Matthew has about seeking for signs (Matt 12:28-42;
Luke 11:29-32). Although he has been keeping very closely to Matthew's
wording, there is a significant difference in the references to the sign of Jonah
in the two gospels: in Matthew it is the sign of Jonah being "three days and three
nights in the belly of the whale," although the consequence is that "the men of
Nineveh . . . repented at the preaching of Jonah." Luke's text, with its closer
parallel between "the queen of the south" and the Ninevites, is clearly more
primitive. Stendahl, speaking of a "School of Matthew"[22] was right in seeing a
secondary editing at Matt 12:40; Luke preserves the text in Matthew as it was
at the time he read that Gospel.

Luke appends two sayings (11:33-36) which have also been inserted into
Matthew's Sermon on the Mount (Matt 5:15; 6:22-23) that light is given us to
see by, fitting these in at what seems an appropriate place. Christ is revealed by
the light of truth, and those with sight must not seek for signs. The condemnation
of the Pharisees and lawyers follows; it has a different context from the corresponding text of Matthew (23:1-36) with Jesus dining at a Pharisee's house; it
is also shorter than Matthew's text. It is noticeably less close to Matthew's

---

[22]Krister Stendahl, *The School of St. Matthew and Its Use of the Old Testament*, Acta
Seminarii neotestamentici Upsaliensis 20, 2nd ed. (Lund: Gleerup, 1968; Philadelphia:
Fortress Press, 1968; [1]1954); see p. 53.

wording than the preceding passages; and it varies in its order. It would seem that Luke has a different source on which he has drawn.

Luke 12:1-12. Fearless Confession. With a fresh context, which like the text itself suggests Luke has a source more or less parallel to Matthew (though in effect he covers Matt 10:26-33, still leaving Matt 10:34-39 unaccounted for), Luke goes on to an exhortation to fearless confession. The link with what has preceded, which may come from a continuous source, is provided by the words of warning against "the leaven of the Pharisees, which is hypocrisy." The connection as Luke sees it seems to be, not that the disciples should avoid hypocrisy in themselves, but be aware that whatever they say will be public knowledge, so they must not fear those who would kill the body. Through the leaven of the Pharisees they will be brought "before the synagogues, and the rulers and the authorities."

Luke 12:13-48. Stewardship. Concern over worldly things is the next subject. It begins with the parable of the Rich Fool (12:13-21): so foolish is "he that layeth up treasure for himself and is not rich towards God." This non-Matthæan pericope leads appropriately to the insertion of a long passage (12:22-34) with a parallel in Matthew's Sermon on the Mount (Matt 6:19-33, except for 6:22-23 which has already been used). Because it is an insertion from a different context, and not a continuation of the words preceding it, it is introduced by a new rubric: "And he said to his disciples." It is followed by an exhortation to watchfulness in the service of Christ (12:35-38), somewhat similar to Matthew's parable of the Ten Virgins but taken from a different source. The nature of the source is indicated by the words ἀμὴν λέγω ὑμῖν, not part of Luke's editorial style, and by the Jewish division of the night into three watches (12:38) as against the Roman division of the night into four (as in Mark 6:48; 13:35). Then again a passage on the same subject, which has probably been added to Proto-Matthew (Matt 24:43-51), is used almost word for word, and a short parable on the servant's punishment or reward is added (12:47-48).

Luke 12:49-59. Days of Decision. The following section (12:49-56), illuminating as showing that Luke's other sources sometimes overlap with Matthew, has already been commented on. It is followed by a short section (12:57-59) a parallel to which, though not in identical words, has been inserted into Matthew's Sermon on the Mount (Matt 5:25-26).

Luke 13:1-21. God's Ways with Men, and Two Parables. From this point until 18:14 Luke seems to be much less dependent on Matthew, both for material, and inevitably now that he has taken so much from Matthew's text, for order also. There follow sections on Repentance (13:1-9) and on the healing of the woman with a spirit of infirmity (13:10-17); and then the parables of the Mustard Seed and Leaven (13:18-21), the twin parables which the editor of Matthew has inserted (Matt 13:31-35) between the parable of the Tares and its interpretation. It is not very obvious why Luke chose to put them in this place, nor indeed why Matthew's editor put them just where he did.

Luke 13:22-35. Looking towards Jerusalem. The thought of Jerusalem, and the consequent reminder that the end of Jesus' ministry would be the Passion there is the link that binds the next three passages. The first begins with the words "and he went on his way through cities and villages, teaching and journeying on to Jerusalem." This might be an insertion of Luke's for editorial purposes, but the fact that the following words (13:23-30) down to the closing logion "There are last which shall be first and there are first which shall be last" (cf. Matt 19:30; 20:16) form a unit, and are not very close to the wording of the parallels scattered in Matthew's Gospel (7:13-14; 25:10-12; 19:30) suggests that they were taken from a different source. But clearly Luke does "cover" this material in Matthew in consequence.

The second of the three connected passages is peculiar to Luke (13:31-33) and is continuous with the first, in that it begins "in that very hour," and we have seen how consistent Luke is in his care not to create false contexts either of time or place. The natural conclusion is that Luke derived this passage from the same source as the preceding one, as continuous with it. Its position here depends on its warning "It cannot be that a prophet perish out of Jerusalem"; it is not meant to give chronological information about when Jesus left Herod's dominions.

The third passage (13:34-35) is paralleled in Matthew (23:37-39), and its insertion by Luke at this point with its cry "Jerusalem, Jerusalem" is almost inevitable here; it is at least as appropriate as in Matthew's text, if Luke found it there.

Luke 14:1-24. Invitations to Meals. There follow two episodes linked together at the beginning by Jesus being at a dinner (14:1-14), followed by the parable of the Great Supper. Only the parable corresponds with anything in Matthew (22:1-10), but the differences are so great that Luke must have taken it from another source.

Luke 14:25–17:21. Independent Narratives. The passage on the cost of discipleship (14:25-35) and the parables of the Lost Sheep, Lost Coin, and Lost Son, and of the Unjust Steward do not seem to owe anything to Matthew. After them, Luke works in sayings that have parallels in Matthew (Luke 16:16-18; Matt 11:12-13; 19:9) on the Law and Divorce, but it is doubtful whether Luke is now dependent on Matthew for any of his material up to 17:21, in spite of verbal similarities. But while the separate sayings of 17:1-6 (on Offences, Forgiveness, and Faith) differ from Matthew's text, the parallels in Matthew (18:6-7; 18:21-22; 17:20) suggest that Luke is now looking again at Matthew's order, to which he is shortly to return (Luke 18:15; Matt 19:13).

Luke 17:22–18:14. The Day of the Son of Man, and Two Parables. The words of 17:20, of Jesus being asked "when the kingdom of God cometh" lead to the inclusion of the speech to the disciples, a version of which has been incorporated by Matthew into the last of his compound discourses. At one point Luke's version is longer; his inclusion of "the days of Lot" as parallel to "the days of Noah" and its contrast with "the day of the Son of man" (as against

Matthew's "parousia of the Son of man") suggest that it copies an early form of the speech. The references to days "when ye shall desire to see one of the days of the Son of man"—by which Luke presumably means one of the days like those of his ministry—and the reference to the coming Passion and the urgency of fleeing from the impending catastrophe do not seem to look forward beyond the future destruction of Jerusalem. In Matthew the material is associated with more apocalyptic prophecies.

Finally, before returning to Matthew's order, Luke adds two parables, those of the Unjust Judge and the Pharisee and the Publican. Luke's rearrangement of Matthew's material between 9:51 and 18:14 has enabled him to do two things: to present the teaching of Jesus in a continuous account and to add material from other sources to what he has drawn from Matthew. Luke has made no attempt at chronological order, or to plot the course of a journey. Now as he comes to the actual approach to Jerusalem, he must go back to Matthew's order, and as he will now be concerned with an actual journey, he will be able to give place names such as Jericho and Olivet.

Luke 18:14–21:38. Back to Matthew, with Omissions and Additions. Having already spoken on Divorce, Luke omits Matt 19:1-12 and then follows Matthew's order until he reaches Matthew's last great discourse (Matt 24:4–25:46) so closely that we need only note his omissions and additions.

Three parables are absent from Luke: The Laborers in the Vineyard (Matt 20:1-16), the Two Sons (Matt 21:28-32), and the Marriage Feast (Matt 22:1-14), the last of these having been already covered by a different version in Luke 14:20-24. Luke also omits the request of the two sons of Zebedee (Matt 20:20-28), most of the details of the cleansing of the temple (Matt 21:10-17), and the whole episode of the cursing of the barren fig tree (Matt 21:18-22) which in Matthew follows immediately. The question of the Great Commandment (Matt 22:34-40) Luke has already dealt with, as he has also the condemnation of the Pharisees (Matt 23:1-36). Luke does however give a short indication of it here, and includes the condemnation of those "who devour widows' houses, and for a pretense make long prayers" (20:47) which is not in Matthew but leads to Luke's own story of the Widow's Mite. The condemnation of Jerusalem (Matt 23:37-39) Luke already has included, probably from a non-Matthæan source.

Luke's additions consist of the story of Zacchaeus (19:1-10), which comes naturally at the point where Jesus is at Jericho; and immediately before returning to Matthew's text, the parable of the Pounds (19:11-27), a variant of Matthew's parable of the Talents (Matt 25:14-30); then the prediction of the destruction of Jerusalem (19:41-44); and the story of the Widow's Mite (21:1-4), characteristic of his concern for widows.

The editor of Matthew has collected a mass of apocalyptic material into the last of his five great discourses (Matt 24, 25), some of this probably not yet included in the text of Matthew available to Luke, but he has already used more or less equivalent material for much of this and for two parables, the Ten Virgins and the Talents, contained in it. Luke therefore has a much shorter parallel to this section, beginning with a warning against deceivers who would proclaim that "the end is at hand"; and adding that before the end comes there will be persecution for Christ's followers, persecution that will bring the opportunity to witness to him (21:13). The siege of Jerusalem is foretold, and the signs that will precede the coming of the Son of man. The parable of the fig tree provides a warning to disciples to be ready to stand before him (21:5-36).

Jesus has arrived at Jerusalem and the whole long teaching section of the Gospel of Luke is brought to an end with a summary: "And every day he was teaching in the temple; and every night he went out, and lodged in the mount that is called Olivet. And all the people came early in the morning to him in the temple, to hear him" (21:37-38).

If, as Evans says of the central part of Luke's Gospel, "the commentators have been at a loss what to make of it,"[23] that is largely because they have sought for the answer in the use that Luke has been supposed to make of Mark and the hypothetical Q. If that part of the Gospel seems to be something of a labyrinth, there is an Ariadne's thread available to guide us through it: it is the use Luke has made of Matthew in the form in which he knew that Gospel.

"Until the day in which he was received up"

The Exodus Jesus was to accomplish at Jerusalem (9:31), "the days of his assumption" (9:51), include the Passion, Resurrection, and Ascension. We have first to compare the story of the Passion as told by Luke and by Matthew in order to make some assessment of Luke's dependence on the other. There are three factors that can help us: the correspondence between them in actual content, in the order in which it is presented, and in the wording.

As regards content, there are several passages in Matthew that have no parallel in Luke. At the beginning of the Passion narrative, Matthew records the anointing at Bethany (a different story from that of the anointing in Luke 7:36-38), and he also records the death of Judas, which Luke was to do in Acts (1:18-19) Both of these were probably additions to Proto-Matthew. Nor does Luke include the mockery of the Roman soldiers (Matt 27:31), speaking instead of that by Herod's soldiers (Luke 23:11);[24] nor the crown of thorns. He does not include the opening of the tombs (Matt 27:51-53) nor the setting of a guard on the tomb (Matt 27:62-63).

There is a difference in order because Luke has a notable addition to Matthew's narrative in the account of the sending of Jesus by Pilate to Herod

---

[23]C. F. Evans, "The Central Section of St Luke's Gospel" in *Studies in the Gospels: Essays in Memory of R. H. Lightfoot*, ed. D. E. Nineham (Oxford: Blackwell, 1955) 30.

[24]See Pierre Benoit, "The Trial of Jesus" in *Jesus and the Gospel*, vol. 1, trans. Benet Weatherhead (London: Darton, Longman, and Todd, 1973) 128-29.

(Luke 23:6-12). This has been criticized as an unlikely occurrence, but the reference to "Johanna the wife of Herod's steward" (8:2; 24:10) and to "Manaen a member of the court of Herod the tetrarch" (Acts 13:1) suggest Luke might have special sources of information. The same association of Herod and Pontius Pilate is made again by Luke in Acts 4:27. That Luke's account of the trials is based on good information is supported by the fact that in another respect his order of events is to be preferred to that of Matthew (and of Mark following Matthew). According to Matthew Jesus was tried at night, and therefore illegally, by Caiaphas and a gathering of the scribes and elders (Matt 26:57), and judgment was given against him. Then in the morning they again "took counsel against Jesus to put him to death." But according to Luke Jesus was taken at night "unto the high priest's house" where he was mocked by the men who were holding him, and it was only in the morning that the Sanhedrin met together and Jesus was condemned. This is supported by John's Gospel, which says Jesus was taken to Annas "the high priest," as he obviously was still commonly called; Jesus was questioned by Annas, and "one of the officers" first struck him. "Annas then sent him to Caiaphas the high priest"—"the high priest that year" as John accurately calls him for distinction. Luke and John support each other and give a much more probable sequence of events.[25] There is therefore, as Benoit says, "no difficulty in thinking that Luke owes his better arrangement of things to an original tradition. It seems to be established, by many other indications, that he had at his disposal, especially for the Passion, a personal source, distinct from Mark, with the help of which he corrects Mark."[26] (It is of course my thesis here that it was not Mark but Matthew whose Gospel was "corrected" by Luke.)

There are other points of agreement between Luke and John that suggest there were details of tradition they had in common.[27] And it is noteworthy these details are such as do not imply that John used Luke. John has added details not in Luke, but these point to special knowledge. Both John and Luke, for example, say the servant in the garden lost his right ear; John alone adds that his name was Malchus (19:10) a detail that has no significance unless it points to actual reminiscence. While both John and Luke say that no man had ever lain in Jesus' tomb, John adds that it was in a garden near Calvary.

As regards wording, Luke has a fairly close correspondence with Matthew, but many of the words and phrases that are identical are such as could hardly be avoided in an account of the Passion: for example, "the mount of Olives," "the cock crew," "Art thou the king of the Jews?" In general Luke follows Matthew's order pretty closely, rewriting much of the narrative in his own style, as he has

---

[25]See Benoit, "Jesus before the Sanhedrin" in *Jesus and the Gospel* for fuller discussion.

[26]Ibid., 1:154.

[27]Cf. Vincent Taylor, *The Formation of the Gospel Tradition*, 2nd ed. (London: Macmillan; New York: St. Martin's, 1935; [1]1933) 53n.1.

done earlier in the Gospel. But it is noticeable that there is not the same identity of wording in the speech of Jesus and of others we might expect from Luke's practice elsewhere, and it is a fair inference that, while using Matthew as a main source, Luke has also used an independent tradition.

Luke's narrative of the Resurrection (24:1-11) corresponds to Matt 24:1-10, but does not seem to depend on it. After that, the canonical text of Matthew concludes with two more short pericopes (28:11-20), the bribing of the soldiers and the final commission. These are absent from Luke, and appear to be additions to Matthew's text as Luke knew it. Luke's own final section (24:13-53) gives the impression, like the Infancy narratives, of being written more freely, that is, without written sources copied.

Already however, in the account of the women at the tomb, Luke shows what is a major purpose in his writing: the necessity of the death of Jesus and the fulfillment of the Old Testament. So in that account we have the words "Remember how he spake unto you when he was yet in Galilee, saying that the Son of man must be delivered up into the hands of sinful men, and be crucified, and the third day rise again" (24:6-7). In the following story of the walk to Emmaus the same point is made: "Behooved it not the Christ to suffer these things, and to enter into his glory? And beginning from Moses and all the prophets, he interpreted to them in all the scriptures the things concerning himself" (24:26-27). Then there follows the narrative of the appearance to the eleven, with the same teaching reiterated: "These are my words which I spake unto you, while I was yet with you, how that all things must needs be fulfilled, which are written in the law of Moses, and the prophets, and the psalms, concerning me. Thus it is written, that the Christ should suffer, and rise again from the dead the third day" (24:44-48). On the occasion of each revelation of the Resurrection the necessity of the Christ's death and the fulfillment of the Scriptures are emphasized.

Finally in three short verses Luke closes his volume with the Ascension in what I have called as regards style a "dismissal," and with an inclusion also, as the disciples return to Jerusalem and to the temple, the place where the Gospel story began.

Conclusions

We have been under no necessity to resort to Mark or to the hypothetical Q in order to follow Luke's thought. In his use of Matthew's Gospel, and with his avowed plan of development, we can see the justification of his own claim to have written "in order." He could not have made such use of Matthew unless he regarded that Gospel as reliable and faithful to the apostolic tradition, but his omission of matters of Palestinian reference suggests that he judged that Matthew did not entirely meet the needs of the readers he had in mind. Some of Luke's other omissions result from the fact that the text of Matthew when Luke wrote did not yet contain everything we now have in the canonical Matthew.

The form of Matthew, with its beginning at the Baptism and with its emphasis on the teaching of Jesus, may well have suggested Luke's overall pattern. The existence of passages in almost identical words and of other parallel sections with widely different wording (always a problem on the Q hypothesis) has a natural explanation if Luke had available both Matthew and other overlapping sources.

Chapter 4

The Writing of the Gospel

To write unto thee. . . .   —Luke 1:3

Luke is, as has often been said, the most literary of the Gospels, written with a sense of style. And if "the style is the man," it should be possible to get some idea of the personality and the purpose of Luke from his manner of writing. His style is in fact a varying one: we have the classical form of the Preface to the Gospel (1:1-4), with the secondary preface of Acts, separated from the Gospel as a second volume, as was necessary, if for on other reason, because of the limited length possible for ancient scrolls.[1] It is followed by the "scriptural" style of the first chapters, in the tradition of the Greek Old Testament. Then there is the careful manner in which Luke edits texts which he has already found in Matthew or other sources, including the direct speech which has to be treated conservatively, lest its meaning is distorted. Again there is the narrative style in which, for example, he describes the final voyage and shipwreck of Paul in the Acts. We have to deal with a writer who is at home in the culture of his day, to whom also the Old Testament is part of his literary as well as religious inheritance, and who writes with responsibility as an editor and with skill as an original author.

It is possible, as has been sometimes suggested, that Matthew's Gospel is in its actual form arranged for lectionary use, but it is unlikely that this was the purpose of Luke's arrangement; the less likely since his second volume would not meet the same need. Luke has written a two volume work for readers, of whom Theophilus is the representative. Its meaning appears, not only in the separate parts, but in the development of his theme from the start to finish. That development accounts, both in the Gospel and in the Acts, both for what is included and what is omitted.

It is our immediate task to take notice of some of the characteristics of Luke's writing which throw light on the meaning and structure of his Gospel. We

---

[1]Cf. H. J. Cadbury, "Commentary on the Preface of Luke," appendix C in pt. 1, vol. 2 of *The Beginnings of Christianity*, ed. F. J. Foakes Jackson and Kirsopp Lake (London: Macmillan, 1922) 496.

can start with one word. The first word of the Gospel, after the preface of 1:1-4, is ἐγένετο ("there was"), and after the introduction of Zacharias and Elizabeth it occurs again in 1:8 in a particular usage ("It came to pass that . . . ") which recurs with frequency in the Gospel, to mark greater or lesser divisions of the text. There are altogether about forty such uses in Luke (two of which are copied in Mark 1:9 and 2:23), and about a dozen in Acts. They are frequent in the first two chapters (Luke 1:8, 23, 41, 59; 2:1, 6, 15, 46), and in the Resurrection stories (24:4, 15, 30, 51), the two parts of the Gospel which would appear to be Luke's own writing without the use of manuscript sources. The usage is discontinued in the Passion narrative, which has its own continuity, as also in the continuous narrative of the latter part of the Acts, until it reappears at 28:8 and 17. The phrase gives the writing a biblical flavor, and in the main body of the Gospel it enables Luke to say that an incident occurred at a particular time (as in 9:28: "It came to pass about eight days after these sayings"); or at a particular place (as in 19:29: "And it came to pass when he drew nigh unto Bethphage"); or merely to give the context of an incident (as in 14:1: "And it came to pass when he went into the house of one of the rulers").

This is important, because the way in which Luke begins particular pericopes, either with this phrase or without it, shows that he never invents his contexts; and notable that if he re-arranges material from Matthew, he is careful not to copy notes of time or occasion which would cease to be accurate. For example, where Matthew has the cure of a leper after the Sermon on the Mount ("And when he was come down from the mountain, there came to him a leper," 8:1-2), and Luke relates the same cure at a different point, he simply says "And it came to pass when he was in one of the cities," without specifying when this was. So also when Luke re-arranges the order in which he recounts the plucking of corn on the sabbath, and when Matthew had written "At that time," Luke merely begins "Now it came to pass on a sabbath,"[2] and when Matthew continued "And he departed thence and went into their synagogue," Luke simply says "And it came to pass on another sabbath" avoiding any suggestion that the two incidents have a chronological position in his Gospel (Luke 6:1, 6; Matt 12:1, 9). Or again, whereas Matthew introduces the parable of the Sower with the words "On that day Jesus went out of the house, and sat by the seaside" (13:1), Luke does so by simply saying, in agreement with Matthew's following words, "And when a great multitude came together, and they of every city resorted unto him" (8:4). On the other hand, when Luke is preserving Matthew's own sequence, as from Matt

---

[2] The reading σαββάτῳ δευτεροπρώτῳ, "second-first sabbath" is to be rejected on the textual evidence. Cf. Plummer's commentary in loc. It is not the kind of language Luke would use, to the mystification of his readers.

16:13 to 17:23 (Luke 9:18-45), he finds no difficulty in including notes of time (9:28: "about eight days after";[3] 9:37 "on the next day").

At his first reference to persons or places, Luke is careful to say whom or what he is talking about. He introduces his characters, and when he refers to places explains what they were. Examples are numerous: "There was in the days of Herod, king of Judaea, a certain priest named Zacharias" (1:8); both the names of Herod and of Zacharias are qualified by explanations. Or, "he came down to Capernaum, a city of Galilee" (4:31); "a city called Nain" (7:11); "a man called by name Zacchaeus" (19:2); " the mount that is called of Olives" (19:29). Matthew is in general less careful, or thought it unnecessary; Mark takes very much more for granted. Luke, at the beginning of the story of the healing of the paralytic at Capernaum (5:17-26) tells us that "there were Pharisees and doctors of the law sitting by"; whereas it is only after Jesus says to the Paralytic "Thy sins are forgiven" that Mark inserts "But there were certain of the scribes sitting there"(2:6). It is indeed only after Luke has defined these as "doctors of the law" that he begins to use the title "scribes" (5:21). Again, in the episode of the man with the withered hand (6:6-11), Luke logically tells us at the beginning that "the scribes and Pharisees watched him," and later says "and they were filled with madness"; Mark, on the other hand, following Matthew and interpreting Matthew's "they asked him," as referring to the Pharisees, begins with "they watched him," and only later specifies who "they" were—"the Pharisees went out." In the story of the Gerasene demoniac, Luke tells us at the beginning that "for a long time he had worn no clothes" (8:27); Mark fails to reproduce this, but adds at the end of the episode that the people found the demoniac "clothed" (Mark 5:15); the matter is not mentioned by Matthew at either point. It often appears that Mark expects his readers to be familiar with a story already.

This is particularly true with regard to the beginning of the Gospel. There are various questions which Mark leaves unanswered, some of them perhaps because he had made no use of the Infancy stories. Who was John the Baptist? Mark baldly says "John came," without explanation (1:4). What was Jesus' connection with Nazareth? Mark 1:9 simply says "Jesus came from Nazareth of Galilee." What happened at the Temptation? Mark 1:12-13 hardly does more than refer to it. Why was John imprisoned? In Mark 1:14 we simply read "Now after John was delivered up." Luke, more adequately than either Matthew or Mark, both of whom answer the last question much later in the Gospel, provides an answer to them all as he brings his characters on to the stage. Instructed Christians would no doubt be able to supply the answers, but Luke's artistry leads him to make adequate introductions.

Apart from deeper considerations arising out of their subject matter it can be seen on stylistic grounds that the first two chapters of Luke are integral to his

---

[3]Matthew actually has "after six days," but Luke's phrase merely means "about a week." Cf. John 20:26.

Gospel. It was part of Streeter's argument in *The Four Gospels*[4] that the existing
Gospel is an enlargement of a "Proto-Luke," that Luke 3:1 looked like the beginning of a book. So he wrote: "This reads . . . as if it was originally written as the
opening section of a book." In fact there is nothing unusual in a dating being
given later than at the beginning of a book, and at a point where the author could
be precise. The first two chapters are necessary introductions to what follows.
The very sentence which begins with the dating that so impressed Streeter
continues with the words "the word of God came unto John the son of Zacharias
in the wilderness," and in the phrase alone there are three things that refer back
to chapters 1 and 2. "John" would be, to Luke, most uncharacteristically
mentioned without any explanation, if this were indeed the first reference to
him;[5] "the son of Zacharias" refers back to 1:80, the only place where there is
any indication how John came to be there. So also in 3:21 our Lord is quite
incidentally mentioned, in the words "Jesus came," on his first appearance after
the first two chapters. So we have too the references to "Joseph" in 4:22 (though
this would be possible as a first reference, as the name occurs in the genealogy,
3:23); to "Galilee" in 4:12, a district which has not been mentioned, except in
3:1 Herod's title as "tetrarch of Galilee"; and to "Nazareth where he had been
brought up" in 4:16—without explanation except that provided in the first two
chapters. On the other hand, when in 4:31 we first hear of Capernaum (apart
from the quotation in direct speech in 4:23) it is defined as "a city of Galilee,"
as was Nazareth on its first mention in 1:26. Such details all point to the first
two chapters being necessary to the integrity of the Gospel, a necessity which
will be confirmed as we turn to the treatment of the apostolic tradition.

As Cadbury has said, "almost studied variation of phrase and exchange of
synonyms is a distinct feature of the style"[6] of Luke, which results in pairs of
words. Whether consciously or unconsciously, Luke likes to balance one thing
against another, and this at all levels. It can be in the balance of two words, such
as "commandments and ordinances" (1:6), "joy and gladness" (1:14), or two
events, like the annunciations to Zacharias and to Mary. It may lead him to
preserve parallel messages, such as the pair of parables of the Mustard Seed and
the Leaven, which Matthew has also preserved; or the double series of beatitudes
and woes (6:20-26) where Matthew has only beatitudes; or the division between
the woes to Pharisees and lawyers (11:39-52), which is not made by Matthew.

---

[4]B. H. Streeter, *The Four Gospels. A Study of Origins, Treating of the Manuscript
Tradition, Sources, Authorship, and Dates* (London: Macmillan, 1924ff.; New York: St.
Martin's Press, 1956ff.) 209.

[5]A remarkable exception is Simon Peter, first mentioned in 4:38. Was his name
already a household word to the readers?

[6]"Four Features of Lucan Style," in *Studies in Luke-Acts: Essays Presented in Honor
of Paul Schubert*, ed. Leander E. Keck and J. Louis Martyn (Nashville: Abingdon, 1966)
92.

There are moreover parallels between the Gospel and Acts. Pentecost corresponds to the Baptism of Jesus in the Gospel; the progression from Nazareth to Galilee and then to Jerusalem is similar to that from Jerusalem to Judaea and Samaria and at last to Rome. In details, the death of Stephen, for instance, has features which recall the death of Jesus; the centurion of Acts 10 reminds us of the centurion of Luke 7. Different passages are linked together, either through some similarity of subject or merely through the use of favorite phrases.[7]

The clearest examples of close parallelism come in the two parts of the Gospel, the Infancy and the Resurrection narratives, where it would seem that Luke was writing most freely, so far as the wording was concerned. The following are of particular interest.

The Two Annunciations (1:11-20; 1:28-37)

1.The Angel's Appearing

And there appeared to him an angel of the Lord, standing on the right side of the altar of incense.	And he came in to her and said, Hail, thou that art highly favored, the Lord is with thee.

2. Fear

And Zacharias was troubled when he saw him, and fear fell upon him.	But she was greatly troubled at the saying, and cast in her mind what manner of salutation this might be.

3. Reassurance

But the angel said unto him, Fear not, Zacharias.	And the angel said unto her, Fear not, Mary.

4.Reason for Reassurance

for thy supplication is heard.	for thou hast found favor with God.

5. The Message

and thy wife Elizabeth shall bear thee a son,	And behold thou shalt conceive in thy womb and bear a son,

6. The Name

and thou shalt call his name John.	and thou shalt call his name Jesus.

7. Description of the Child

And thou shalt have joy and gladness, and many shall rejoice at his birth, for he shall be great . . . to make ready for the Lord a people prepared.	He shall be great, and shall be called the Son of the Most High . . . and of his kingdom there shall be no end.

---

[7]Cadbury, "Commentary on the Preface of Luke," gives numerous examples of verbal similarities.

8. The Question

And Zacharias said unto the angel, Whereby shall I know this?	And Mary said unto the angel, How shall this be?

9. Reason for the Question

For I am an old man, and my wife well stricken in years.	seeing I know not a man.

10. The Answer

And the angel answering said unto him, I am Gabriel . . . these good tidings.	And the angel answered and said unto her, The Holy Ghost shall come upon you . . . the Son of God.

11. The Sign

And behold, thou shalt be silent . . . fulfilled in their season.	And behold, Elizabeth thy kinswoman . . . no word of God shall be void of power.

The correspondence between the two narratives is very close, and incidentally makes the theories sometimes advanced that there have been interpolations into the text of the annunciation to Mary wholly untenable. "If Mary's hesitating question is omitted we destroy the parallelism in structure between the two annunciations."[8] The virginal conception is integral to the narrative.

A similar structure is to be seen in the story of the appearance of the angel to the shepherds at Bethlehem (2:9-12); while not all the eleven elements of the previous scheme are included, the basic similarity is clear. The passage is set out for comparison with the previous ones, with the same numbers as before.

1. The Angel's Appearing
And an angel of the Lord stood before them,
and the glory of the Lord shone round about them.

2. Fear
and they were filled with fear.

3. Reassurance
And the angel said unto them, Fear not.

4. Reason for Reassurance
for behold, I bring you good tidings of great joy,
which shall be to all the people.

5. The Message
for there shall be born to you
this day in the city of David a Savior,

---

[8]John M. Creed, *The Gospel according to St. Luke. The Greek Text with Introduction, Notes, and Indexes* (London: Macmillan, 1930) 14.

6. The Name
which is Christ the Lord.

11. The Sign
And this shall be the sign unto you: Ye shall find a babe
wrapped in swaddling clothes, and lying in a manger.

Two further narratives (25:4-8; 24:36-42) show part of the same pattern.
They deal with two appearances, one of angels, and the other of the risen Lord,
in the final chapter.

The Resurrection (24:4-8; 24:36-42)

1. The Appearance

And it came to pass, while they were perplexed thereabout, behold two men stood before them in dazzling apparel.	And as they spake these things, he himself stood in the midst of them (and said unto them, Peace be unto you).

2. Fear

And as they were affrighted, and bowed down their faces to the earth.	But they were terrified and affrighted, and supposed they beheld a spirit.

3. Reassurance

they said unto them, Why seek ye the living among the dead?	And he said unto them, Why are ye troubled, and why do reasonings arise in your hearts?

5. and 11. The Message and the Sign

[He is not here, but is risen.] Remember how he spake unto you, when he was yet in Galilee, saying that the Son of man must be delivered . . . and on the third day rise.	See my hands and my feet, that it is I myself; handle me and see, for a spirit hath not flesh and bones, as you behold me having.

The words in brackets, omitted in some manuscripts, are probably authentic.
Similar textual questions are raised by the narrative of the institution of the
Eucharist where the longer text represents a parallelism of structure (22:15-20).

The Passover (22:15-18)

And he said unto them;	And he received a cup, and when he had given thanks, he said,
With desire I have desired to eat this passover with you before I suffer; for I say unto you,	Take this, and divide it among yourselves; for I say unto you,
I will not eat it	I will not drink henceforth of the fruit of the vine,
until it be fulfilled in the kingdom of God.	until the kingdom of God shall come.

The Eucharist (22:19-20)

And he took bread, and when he had given thanks, he brake it,

saying, This is my body

which is given for you. This do in remembrance of me.

And the cup in like manner after supper,

saying, This cup is the new covenant in my blood

which is poured out for you.

The parallel structure of these verses gives support to the case for the authenticity of the "longer text" of Luke at this point. It is probable that here, as in the Lucan form of the Lord's Prayer, we have the influence of the liturgical forms with which he was familiar. And incidentally it may be noted that "with desire I have desired" is a Semitism which sounds like genuine reminiscence.

In Cadbury's essay on Lucan style already referred to, he says: "That Luke deliberately avoided repetition seems almost demonstrated by his use of Mark. Mark did not feel the same objection to repetition, but when a word, even the name of an object, occurs too often in his narrative, Luke either by omission or by the use of a synonym secures variety of phrases."[9] He gives a number of examples, of which the following are of special interest.

(1) In Luke 23:53 and 55, 24:1 and 2, the author alternates between the use of the forms μνῆμα and μνημεῖον. This is characteristically Lucan. But although Mark does not avoid repetition, he has a similar variation in his chapter 5. In Mark 5:2 ἐκ τῶν μνημείων is exactly parallel with Matt 8:28, and in 5:3 ἐν τοῖς μνήμασιν is identical with the parallel of Luke 8:27. Mark 5:5 repeats the phrase as he has just used it (and here without parallel in either Matthew or Luke) without variation.

(2) Luke 7:1-10; Matt 8:5-13. We have already noticed that Luke keeps Matthew's παῖς in a quotation of direct speech, but alters it to δοῦλος in his narrative.

(3) Luke 5:17-26; Matt 9:1-8. Matt 9:2 and 6 use κλίνη for "bed." Luke follows Matthew on the first occasion; he varies to κλινιδιόν on the second. After that, with no parallel in Matthew, he varies further to "that on which he lay."[10]

(4) Luke 8:7, 14. In 8:7 Luke has ἀπέπνιξαν, precisely the same as Matt 13:7; Mark has συνέπνιξαν. In 8:14 Luke has συμπνίγονται for Matthew's συμπνίγει Mark has συμπνίγουσιν. Luke's variation is consistent with his using Matthew, and rather less consistent with his following Mark.

---

[9] Cadbury, "Commentary on the Preface of Luke," 93.

[10] Cf. other Lucan paraphrases used for variation: in 19:28 we have "two of the disciples" which in 19:32 becomes "those who were sent" (Matt 21:6 "the disciples"; in 23:18 "Barabbas" which in 23:25 becomes "the man who had been thrown into prison for insurrection and murder, whom they asked for" (Matt 27:26 "Barabbas").

(5) Luke 9:5; 10:11. In Luke 9:5, where as we have seen he is following Matthew in order and subject, he has τὸν κονιορτὸν ἀπὸ ποδῶν ὑμῶν ἀποτινάσσετε corresponding closely to Matthew's ἐκπνάξατε τὸν κονιορτὸν τῶν ποδῶν ὑμῶν. In 10:11, where there is good reason for believing that he is following a different source for the mission of the Seventy, he has τὸν κονιορτὸν τὸν κολληθέντα . . . εἰς τοὺς πόδας ἀπομασσόμεθα. It may not be a stylistic variation of his own.

(6) Luke 9:10, 18. Luke varies from κατ' ἰδίαν in 9:10 to κατὰ μόνας in 9:18; but 9:10 is parallel to κατ' ἰδίαν in Matt 14:13; 9:18 is without parallel.

The first of these six examples suggests that Mark 5:2, 3 conflates Matthew and Luke. The others all point to Luke having used Matthew.

That Luke liked variety of expression, even when it was not represented in his sources, it not without significance. I take as an example a passage close to Matthew's parallel, but without parallel in Mark (Luke 12:42-46; Matt 24:45-50). Here Matthew uses the same word δοῦλος for "servant" four times. For the first of these Luke substitutes the word οἰκονόμος, "steward," a fair interpretation of the meaning of "servant" in Matthew's text. For the second, Luke copies Matthew's "that servant," δοῦλος ἐκεῖνος, and therefore cannot alter the word, when the same phrase recurs twice, without spoiling the balance of the wording. But Matthew also has συνδούλους, "fellow-servants"; Luke again feels freer; and writes παῖδας καὶ τὰς παιδίσκας, "menservants and maidservants." It is clear that in reckoning the degree of identity between a text of Matthew and one of Luke, allowance has to be made for Luke's stylistic variations. It brings their texts significantly closer to each other. In this same passage Luke's ἀληθῶς is clearly only a translation of Matthew's ἀμήν.

The style of Luke 1:1-4 shows that the author could write in a very different way from that which he regarded as appropriate for the rest of the Gospel. In that, he kept closer to the style of his sources. There is however a distinction to be drawn between the comparative freedom he allowed himself in re-casting narrative and the care he exercised in keeping, apart from minor stylistic changes, to the text of the spoken word, and especially of the words of Jesus. As a Christian writing for Christians, there were forms of expression that came naturally to him in his narrative. So for example he could speak of "apostles" (as at 9:10) and even when Matthew had used "disciples" (Matt 17:9; 26:27; 28:7; Luke 17:; 22:14; 24:10); it was the language of the Church of his day. So in his narrative Luke could call Jesus "the Lord," though it is noticeable that after the Introduction of chapters 1-3. and apart from one instance at Nain (7:13), the occurrences are all in the latter part of the Gospel (10:1; 11:39; 12:42; 13:15; 17:5; 17:6; 18:6; 19:8; 22:61; 24:3; 24:34; and possibly 22:31), all without parallels in Matthew. The one instance where the title Lord is taken from Matthew is in 19:31 and 34 (Matt 21:3) where it is taken from direct speech, and its meaning is ambiguous.

Luke freely used "the Lord" in narrative, but he is more cautious in the use of the vocative κύριε as a form of address. Matthew regularly uses this, and sometimes διδάσκαλε, "teacher" as the equivalent of the Aramaic Rabbi. It is clear from Matt 8:19 and 21, and 23:8 that both κύριε and διδάσκαλε are for him equivalent translations of this. No doubt he was conscious that the word κύριε could suggest more, and this is perhaps the reason why he avoided it when recording the words of the betrayer (26:2, 49) and then kept the untranslated Rabbi. Luke is more discriminating, with a sense of the deeper significance of the title. Apart from three or possibly four occasions (Luke 5:12; 7:6; 9:59?; 18:41), where Luke has taken over κύριε from Matthew, the only occasions when he uses κύριε as an address are when this is on the lips of one of Jesus' followers (including Zacchaeus and Martha), or would-be followers. At 8:24 and 9:33 he changes Matthew's κύριε to ἐπιστάτα, "Master," and at 9:38 to διδάσκαλε, "Teacher." Matthew never has ἐπιστάτα, but when Matthew has διδάσκαλε, and Luke also includes a form of address (Matt 19:16; 22:16; 22:24; 22:36; Luke 18:18; 20:1; 20:28; 10:25) he keeps Matthew's "Teacher"; in the same way he keeps Matthew's "The Teacher says" (Matt 26:18) at 22:11. Jesus as Lord is the theme of Acts rather than of the Gospel, and Luke is conscious of its significance for Christians. His usage also illustrates his dependence on Matthew.

The endings of Luke's narratives are as significant as his openings. They may be grouped under four heads: dismissal, climaxes, summaries, end-pieces.

(1) At the close of an episode as Luke recounts it, there is in almost every instance where the subject-matter allows it, what may be called a *dismissal* of characters. That is so, for example, in every one of the Infancy narratives, the relevant words of which are as follows:

> the message to Zacharias: "he departed to his house" (1:23), and "she hid herself" (1:24);
> the Annunciation: "and the angel departed from her" (1:38);
> the Visitation: "And Mary returned unto her house" (1:56);
> the birth of John: "and the child . . . was in the deserts till the day of his showing unto Israel" (1:80);
> the birth of Jesus: "and the shepherds returned" (2:20);
> the presentation in the temple: "they returned unto Galilee to their own city Nazareth" (2:39);
> the Passover visit: "And he went down with them and came to Nazareth" (2:51).

Similar examples can be found throughout the Gospel. The following are instances.

"He shut up John in prison" (3:20). Luke might even have added at this point "and he put him to death," but as he intends to record John's message he begins "Now when John heard in the prison," but Luke does not need to make the point again, and omits this.

"He departed from him for a season" (4:13). Matthew adds at this point "and behold, angels came and ministered unto him," but Luke's instinct is to close with Satan's departure. Luke's fondness for such dismissals takes away perhaps some of the force of the arguments that have been built on the words "for a season."[11] Apart from the symbolic phrase "I beheld Satan fallen as lightning from heaven" (10:18), Satan does not appear again as a "character" in the story until 22:3, "And Satan entered into Judas," but Jesus can refer to there having been temptations in the interim (22:28).

"And he withdrew himself in the deserts and prayed" (5:16). Matthew, after the healing of a leper, continues that Jesus went into Capernaum (8:5). As Luke has changed the context, he first summarizes the effect of Jesus' healings, that "multitudes came together," and then closes with this dismissal. "Go in peace" (7:50). This is at the end of a story without parallel in the other Gospels.

"And he went his way, publishing throughout the whole city how great things Jesus had done for him" (8:29). Matthew says "all the city came out to meet Jesus, and they besought him that he would depart from their borders" (8:34); Luke ends with his dismissal and avoids this addition.

In Luke's natural variety of style, these dismissals are put in various forms. They may be stated, or as in 7:17 "And this report went forth," implied in another statement; or as in 7:50, "Go in peace," implied in spoken words. They may obviously be compared to the *exit* or *exeunt* of stage plays.

A further point is important for the understanding of certain passages in the Gospel. When Luke has no occasion to refer again to a particular person, he may "dismiss" him immediately, even though his actual departure did not yet occur. For example, after his preaching by the Jordan, John the Baptist was obviously present and active at the Baptism of Jesus (3:31-32), but since Luke does not propose to mention him in the narrative of the Baptism, he immediately dismisses him from the story (3:18-20), by relating his imprisonment, although this was to happen later.

This literary device, of *anticipated dismissals,* may be illustrated at a further point in connection with the Baptist. The infant John could not possibly have gone to a solitary life in the wilderness, and Luke does not mean that he did so. But after his birth he is not to appear in the narrative until the time of his preaching, and Luke therefore leaves him, growing in body and spirit, and going to the wilderness until the word of God should come to him there (3:2).

Similarly in the account of the Visitation, Mary goes to her kinswoman "in the sixth month" and remains with her three months; that brings us to the time of John's birth; the story ends with the "dismissal" of Mary—she "returned unto her home." On this Creed comments: "Mary returns to her home before the birth

---

[11]See Hans Conzelmann, *The Theology of St. Luke,* trans. Geoffrey Buswell (London; New York: Harper, 1960; Philadelphia: Fortress, 1982) 28 and passim.

of Elizabeth's child";[12] and Charles Gore wrote: "One can only wonder why she returned home immediately before the crisis of the birth of Elizabeth's child."[13] The simple explanation of the text is that Mary remained for that birth, for which she had waited three months; but as she is not being named among the neighbors and kinsfolk (1:58), her subsequent departure is dealt with, in an "anticipated dismissal," at this point.

A further example is to be seen in the account of Peter's denial. In Matthew, followed by Mark, Peter is brought to the courtyard, and only after the examination by the high-priest is the story of his denial added. Luke rearranges the material. Having brought Peter to the courtyard he proceeds immediately to the story of his denials, and only after the "dismissal" (in words taken from Matthew) do we return to what was happening to Jesus.

An interesting example of Luke's stylistic methods is to be seen in Acts 11:27-12:25. The passage begins with the famine which would probably be dated in A.D. 46; and with Herod's attack on the Church and his subsequent death in A.D. 44. Superficially it looks as though Luke has put them in the wrong order, but this is to misunderstand his methods. He begins with a favorite biblical phrase, "in those days,"[14] and deals with the subject of the famine, bringing Barnabas and Saul to Jerusalem. He knows that it was about this period, and actually it was rather earlier, that Herod attacked Christians; so at 12:1 he continues with the vague phrase "about that time" to relate the martyrdom of James and the imprisonment of Peter. This brings the narrative to 12:19. At this point Luke makes one of his characteristic dismissals by adding in 12:20-23 the story of Herod's death. The whole narrative referring to Herod is then closed by an inclusion: "But the word of God grew and multiplied." This has no connection with Herod's death, but looks back to 12:1: "now about that time Herod the king put forth his hands to afflict certain of the Church." In effect 12:1-24 is put into brackets. After that the narrative, which left Barnabas and Saul in Jerusalem at 11:30, is resumed at 12:25 with their return. The growth of the home Church has been summarized: "The word of God grew and multiplied," and the book can proceed to Paul's first missionary journey.

The final dismissal of the Gospel is the Ascension, simply recorded, with no note of time, as the Acts is to deal with this more fully as the ground and prelude of the Christian mission. To say that in the Third Gospel the Ascension "takes place on Easter Day itself"[15] is to misunderstand Luke's methods. It is not even necessary to assume that 24:44ff, beginning "And he said unto them"

---

[12]Creed, *The Gospel according to St. Luke*, in loc.

[13]C. Gore, "The Gospel according to St. Luke" in his *A New Commentary on Holy Scripture Including the Apocrypha* (London: SPCK, 1928) in loc.

[14]Cf. Luke 1:39; 2:1; Acts 1:15; 2:18; etc.

[15]Ernst Haenchen, in *Studies in Luke-Acts: Essays Presented in Honor of Paul Schubert*, ed. Keck and Martyn, 260.

(εἶπεν δὲ πρὸς αὐτούς) is meant to refer to the same day as the preceding verses; and even less to assume that the last commission (24:46-49), beginning with a fresh rubric "And he said to them" (καὶ εἶπεν αὐτοῖς) is meant to be given on the same occasion. The final words (24:50-53) simply close the Gospel, leaving further treatment of the Ascension for the next volume. The difference between the Gospel and the Acts corresponds to the different purposes in the development of the two-volume work.

(2) Less significant is the practice which Luke has in common with Matthew and Mark, of ending an episode or narrative with a final sentence of special significance or force, which for convenience may be called a climax. This is the pattern for the form of the pronouncement-stories analyzed by the form-critics. "The Son of Man is lord of the sabbath" (Luke 6:5; Matt 12:8) is a typical example. It is however not only in pericopes which have been preserved as a setting for such sentences that it is natural to end with a memorable saying. Luke for instance uses the warning "Ye cannot serve God and mammon" (16:13) as the close of a section, when Matthew (6:24) merely has it in the context of the Sermon on the Mount. Luke can make equally effective use of the same device in telling a parable, as in 16:31: "If they hear not Moses and the prophets, neither will they be persuaded if one rise from the dead"; or as a comment on a parable: "Go and do thou likewise" (10:37). A similar affect can also be achieved in a story which can hardly have been remembered merely to record its final saying: "Mary hath chosen the good part, which shall not be taken away from her" (10:42). The method is in any case part of the stock-in-trade of any good story-teller.

The desire to give a particular point its full impact may account for Luke's two omissions about St. Peter in the episode recounted by Matthew at Caesarea Philippi. After the proclamation "The Christ of God," for Matthew's "Thou art the Christ, the Son of the living God" (Matt 16:15), Luke omits Matt 16:17-19, continuing immediately with the prophecy of the Passion and Resurrection. He omits the promise and the rebuke to Peter, having made his essential point.

In general, in pronouncement stories the differences between Matthew and Luke are slight, since Luke makes fewer editorial changes when recording direct speech, and especially the words of Jesus, than he does in narrative.

(3) A third characteristic of Luke's style, both in the Gospel and the Acts,[16] is the use of short *summaries*. At different points in the gospel a short summary is given, marking the stage reached in the development of Jesus' life and ministry. So we have:

2:40: "And the child grew, and waxed strong in spirit, filled with wisdom, and the grace of God was upon him";
4:4: "And he was preaching in the synagogues of Judaea";

---

[16]E.g., Acts 2:46-47; 4:4; 6:7.

19:47: "And he was teaching daily in the temple";
21:37: "And every day he was teaching in the temple."

One such summary, of Jesus' ministry in Galilee—"a fame went out concerning him throughout all the region round about, and he taught in their synagogues, being glorified by all" (4:14-15)—serves a double purpose: it justifies the allusion to what Jesus had done at Capernaum (4:23), and as Conzelmann has said, the words "look forward and provide a survey of the whole of the first period of the ministry of Jesus,"[17] Matthew had merely said that Jesus began to preach (4:17).

(4) Even when they are not summaries of the stage reached, especially in the first two chapters, what may be called "endpieces" may be added—short additions to the main body of the narrative, illustrating or completing what has been recorded. Thus at the end of the story of the message to Zacharias, and after the dismissal of Zacharias himself, we have the short note of the conception of Elizabeth (1:24-25); after that of the birth of Jesus, we have the note about his circumcision (2:21); after the account of the anointing in Simon's house, that of the ministering women (8:1-3). Apart from the insertion of Magnificat into the text[18] between 1:45 and 1:56, the narrative of the Visitation can be seen to be, so far as literary form is concerned, an endpiece to that of the Annunciation.

(5) Finally, Luke sometimes makes use of the device of *inclusion,* by which a narrative is brought back to the point from which it began. It can be seen in 4:14-44, which begins "And Jesus returned in the power of the Spirit into Galilee . . . and he taught in their synagogues," and ends "and he was preaching in the synagogues of Judaea."[19] Another example can be seen in 20:1-21:38, which begins "And it came to pass on one of the days, as he was teaching the people in the temple," and closes "And every day he was teaching in the temple, and every night he went out, and lodged in the mount that is called the Mount of Olives. And all the people came early in the morning to him in the temple, to hear him."

"The style is the man." Luke writes with a deep sense of responsibility for the presentation of the truth of the Gospel, with a recognition of its continuity with the Old Testament revelation, with ease in expressing it in literary form, and with a consistent purpose as he follows out his theme. He is an artist, always conscious of the nature of the material on which he worked.

---

[17]Conzelmann, *The Theology of St. Luke,* 30.

[18]See above, 42.

[19]No distinction is meant between "Galilee" and "Judaea." See above, chap. 3, n. 10, and cf. I. Howard Marshall, *Luke, Historian and Theologian* (Exeter: Paternoster Press, 1970; Grand Rapids: Zondervan, 1971) 71.

Chapter 5

Fulfillment in the Gospel

Those things which have been fulfilled among us. . . .　　　　—Luke 1:1

The Essentials of the Gospel

"Luke's Gospel," wrote Dibelius, "contains not the content of the gospel but a guarantee of that content."[1] Luke must indeed have taken for granted that the proclaiming of the gospel was being done by word of mouth by the Christian missionaries; his task was to illustrate and to justify that proclamation, and to build upon that foundation. What then did Luke regard as the basic elements of that gospel? What, so to speak, was his "Apostles' Creed"? It is a question Luke himself helps us answer since in Acts he has written of the early days of preaching. From Luke's own writing we can discern what were in his view the salient features of that proclamation. To the relevant passages in Acts may be added one from the end of the Third Gospel itself (24:46-49), consisting of the words of the risen Christ to his disciples. The passages from the Acts are as follows.

1:1-8. Luke's recapitulation of his first volume.
1:21-22. The requirements for the appointment of a successor to Judas.
2:16-36. Peter's speech at Pentecost.
3:11-26. Peter's speech on Solomon's Porch.
5:30-32. The words of Peter and the Apostles before the Sanhedrin.
10:36-43. The words of Peter in the house of Cornelius.
13:23-41. Part of Paul's address at Antioch of Pisidia.
17:2-3. Paul's preaching at Thessalonica.
17:30-31. Part of Paul's speech at Athens.

The burden of these passages inevitably varies somewhat according to the exigencies of the different contexts, but the elements which make them up are

---

[1]Martin Dibelius, *From Tradition to Gospel*, trans. Bertran Lee Woolf (London: Ivor Robinson and Watson, 1934; New York: Scribner's, 1965; Greenwood SC: Attic, 1982).

remarkably constant. Most of the passages are set out in convenient form in Dodd's *The Apostolic Preaching and Its Developments*,[2] and it is therefore unnecessary to set them out at length here. They would require separate study if we were, for example, comparing the treatment in the speeches of Peter with those of Paul, but for our present purpose in seeing what Luke relates as the gospel proclamation we can look at them as a whole. Nor need we at this stage consider whether the speeches are in any way accurate reporting, or compositions of Luke to provide what he thought appropriate. In either case they give us what Luke regarded as the form of proclaiming the gospel. We can therefore consider the result of conflating them together.

Who Jesus Was. A number of titles are used for Jesus in these passages, various ways of proclaiming the lordship of Christ, which is the heart of the gospel. He is described as God's Son and his Servant, as Lord, as the Holy and Righteous One, and as the Lord of life; but the gospel could not be proclaimed by beginning with such claims, they could only be made as witnessed to by what Jesus was shown to be by his life and deeds. The one claim that could be made about Jesus' origin that could not be disputed, but which would be regarded in Israel as a precondition to all claims of messiahship, was that he was a son of David. So Acts 2:30 speaks of the promise of God to David that "of the fruit of his loins he would set upon his throne," and this passage is set in a larger context dealing with David (2:25-36). Similarly the speech at Antioch has an extended reference to David (13:33-37) and it is recorded that "of this man's seed hath God according to promise brought unto Israel a Savior, Jesus" (13:23).

The Ministry. Behind the claims for Jesus was the evidence of his ministry. John had first preached the baptism of repentance, himself baptizing with water; but he looked forward to one who was to come, the shoes of whose feet he was not worthy to unloose. It was Jesus who came, anointed with the Holy Spirit and with power; he was the Christ, the prophet like unto Moses, and the Savior. Jesus preached repentance and remission of sins; he went about, first in Galilee, but also in all the land of the Jews and in Jerusalem, preaching good tidings of peace. That God was with him was shown because through him God did mighty works and wonders and signs, healing those who were oppressed with the devil. He chose apostles, who were witnesses of all he did; he taught them that the Scriptures must be fulfilled in him.

The Passion and Crucifixion. Jesus was "delivered up," Judas being the guide of them that took him. Those who dwelt at Jerusalem, with their rulers, not knowing Jesus, condemned him to death. He was denied before Pilate, when he was determined to release him; the Jews asked for a murderer to be released to them, and killed the Prince of Life. So by the hands of lawless men Jesus was

---

[2]C. H. Dodd, *The Apostolic Preaching and Its Developments. Three Lectures with an Appendix on Eschatology and History* (London: Hodder & Stoughton, 1936; New York: Harper, 1937).

slain, being crucified. Then he was taken down from the tree and laid in a tomb. Jesus suffered, but it was as the Christ he had to die, in fulfillment of the Scriptures.

The Resurrection. After his passion Jesus was raised from the dead on the third day by "the God of our fathers." The pangs of death were loosed for him, for it was not possible that he should be held by it; his soul was not left in Hades, nor did his flesh see corruption. Jesus showed himself alive by many proofs, appearing to his disciples by the space of forty days.

The Ascension and Exaltation. After the forty days, Jesus was "by the right hand of God exalted"; the apostles had been with him "unto the day that he was received up," now to be a Prince and a Savior; God had said to him "Sit thou on my right hand," glorifying his Servant Jesus.

The Gift of the Holy Spirit. Jesus, who had himself been anointed with the Holy Spirit and with power, told his disciples to tarry in the city until they should be clothed with power from on high; he would send forth the promises of the Father upon them; so "not many days hence" they would be baptized with the Holy Spirit and with power, as happened on the day of Pentecost. The gift of the Holy Spirit was for those who obeyed God; it was Jesus who poured it forth, having received the promise of that Spirit from the Father.

The Witness of the Apostles. The apostles were witnesses of what had happened, and especially of the Resurrection; they had known Jesus from the baptism of John until the day of his Ascension, having seen the risen Lord, who appeared to them by many proofs. As witnesses they had eaten and drunk with the Lord after he rose from the dead. He had given them a command to bear their witness both in Jerusalem, and in all Judea and Samaria and unto the end of the earth, for they were charged to preach to the people. With their witness was associated that of the Holy Spirit himself.

Judgment. Jesus was "ordained by God to be the judge of the living and the dead," and God had "appointed a day, in which he will judge the world in righteousness by the man whom he hath ordained." At the Ascension the apostles were told that Jesus, who had gone from them into heaven, would come in like manner. God would send the Christ, who had been appointed for men, even Jesus "whom the heaven must receive until the times of restoration of all things."

Repentance and Forgiveness. According to the words of the risen Lord to the disciples, "it was written" that repentance and remission of sins should be preached in the name of Christ to all nations, beginning at Jerusalem. This was repeated by Peter in the house of Cornelius when he said, "To him bear all the prophets witness, that through his name every one that believeth on him shall receive remission of sins." So on the day of Pentecost Peter had answered the question "What shall we do?" by saying, "Repent ye, and be baptized every one of you in the name of Jesus Christ, unto the remission of your sins, and ye shall receive the gift of the Holy Spirit"; and in Solomon's Portico he makes the same proclamation: "Repent ye therefore, and turn again, that your sins may be blotted out." Before the Sanhedrin, Peter and the apostles asserted that God had exalted Jesus to be a Prince and a Savior "to give repentance to Israel, and remission of sins." Paul has the same message: "that through this man is proclaimed unto you remission of sins, and by him every one that believeth is justified from all things from which ye could not be justified by the law of Moses." At Athens Paul has the same message: "The times of ignorance God overlooked, but now commandeth men that they should all everywhere repent."

Such, according to Luke's own testimony, were the terms in which the gospel was first proclaimed to his readers; these then were the primary matters about which he was to write "in order." Of his two volumes, the first would begin with the Davidic origin of Jesus and continue to the Ascension, which as the climax of the earthly life of our Lord would be the last recorded event; as the primary event in the life of the Church it would be the first recorded in Acts.

In that second volume Luke was to continue with the remaining items of the kerygma: it might almost be called "The Gospel: Part Two." After relating the Ascension, Acts was to continue with the Gift of the Spirit at Pentecost and the consequent signs of the operation of the Holy Spirit in the life of the Church.

> The fact that the same Spirit which worked in Jesus is now given by him as the exalted Messiah to his followers renders the subsequent history of the Church and its mission parallel, in certain respects, to that of his own life and work. . . . The power of the Spirit thus operates in mighty works through the disciples as it formerly worked through Jesus.[3]

The witness of the apostles necessarily became the most obvious theme of the book, so much so that it came to be called the Acts *of the Apostles.* From the witness, especially of Peter, at Jerusalem, it continues through the extension of the gospel in Judea and Samaria until it passes to the work of Paul, of whom Luke had direct knowledge. The gospel did not in fact only spread westward, but Paul was a link between Jerusalem and Rome, as shown in the words "As thou hast testifed concerning me at Jerusalem, so must thou bear witness also at Rome" (Acts 23:11), Rome being for Luke a representative city for "the uttermost part of the earth."

The themes of Judgment and of Repentance and Forgiveness, which concern the response to the gospel, do not admit of the same treatment, but they are in effect dealt with in the record of acceptance or rejection of the gospel by those to whom it was preached. Insofar as Judgment meant that this would be at a future day, when the world would be judged, it necessarily falls out of the scope of the book.

---

[3]G. W. H. Lampe, "The Holy Spirit in the Writings of St. Luke," in *Studies in the Gospels: Essays in Memory of R. H. Lightfoot,* ed. Dennis E. Nineham (Oxford: Blackwell, 1957) 194-95.

Luke-Acts then is a continuous story in two volumes. It is a mistake to let our own interest in biography and curiosity about the life of Paul lead us to suppose, as has sometimes been done, that a third volume was intended. Acts itself is in three parts, with the preaching of the gospel the subject of each part: at Jerusalem (1–5) with the final words of summary "And every day, in the temple and at home, they ceased not to teach and preach Jesus as the Christ." Acts 6 introduces Stephen, through whom the gospel came to be spread further afield, as Christians "were all scattered throughout the region of Judea and Samaria" (8:1); this second part closes again with a summary (12:24): "the word of God grew and multiplied." Then the final division of the book shows the witness carried into the Gentile world, and to its focus at Rome, where it closes with Paul "preaching the kingdom of God and teaching all things concerning the Lord Jesus Christ quite openly and unhindered." It is irrelevant that the life stories of Peter and Paul are left incomplete; Luke was not writing biography, nor even setting out to show the geographical spread of the Christian faith; he was showing that the witness was being borne to the Gentile world, in which for him Rome was the center. Apart from the characteristic endpiece of Acts 28:30-31, Acts and therefore the whole two-volume work, closes with the solemn proclatation that "the salvation of God is sent to the Gentiles."

Fulfillment in the Apostolic Preaching

According to the preface of Luke, the matters with which it had to deal were those "fulfilled among us." This is indeed the message of Paul, who at the beginning of his letter to the Romans (1:1-2) speaks of "the gospel of God, which he promised afore by his prophets in the holy scriptures." The note of fulfillment runs through the passages of Acts that record the preaching of the apostles. It is "according to promise" that God has brought to Israel a Savior of the seed of David (12:23), and the reference to David in itself implies a fulfillment of the promises of the Old Testament. Jesus came in fulfillment of the words of Moses (3:22-23), and indeed "all the prophets from Samuel and them that followed after, as many as have spoken, they also told of these days" (3:24).

Especially is the idea of fulfillment stressed in connection with the Passion. Behind the promises of Scripture lay the "determinate counsel and foreknowledge of God" (Acts 2:23).[4] In the Scriptures themselves, the fate of Judas was foreshadowed in the Psalms (Acts 1:16, 20); the dwellers at Jerusalem and their rulers fulfilled the voices of the prophets, which they ignored, when they condemned Jesus (13:27). It was when they had fulfilled all things that were written of him that they took him down and laid him in a tomb (13:29). Jesus was the Servant of God, foretold by Isaiah (3:13). So it could be said that the gospel was

---

[4]Cf. Titus 1:2: πρό χρόνων αἰωνίων, literally, and I think intentionally, "before eternal times."

"nothing but what the prophets and Moses did say should come, how that the Christ must suffer" (6:22-23). In preaching the gospel, therefore, Paul, as his custom was . . . reasoned with them from the scriptures, opening and alleging that it behooved the Christ to suffer, and to rise from the dead, and saying that this Jesus, whom I proclaim unto you, is the Christ" (17:2-3). It could all be summed up by saying that "the things which God foreshadowed by the mouth of all the prophets, that his Christ should suffer, be thus fulfilled" (3:18).

It is the same with the Resurrection. It is the fulfillment of what Moses and the prophets have said (26:23) and is bound up with the fulfillment of the prophecies that the Christ should suffer (for example, 17:3). On the day of Pentecost, Peter quotes Psalm 16 at some length, and claims that David foreseeing what would happen to Jesus "spake of the resurrection of the Christ, that neither was he left in Hades, no did his flesh see corruption" (2:31). The same argument is used by Paul at Antioch of Pisidia (16:32-37), summing up the argument by saying, "We bring you good tidings of the promise made unto the fathers, how that God hath fulfilled the same unto us their children, in that he raised up Jesus."

For the Ascension, the classical quotation (made or implied in many places in the New Testament, as it was also to be in the Apostles' Creed and Nicene Creed) is from Psalm 110. It is appealed to in Acts 2:34 where Peter, saying that Jesus was "exalted at the right hand of God," continues: "For David ascended not into the heavens, but he saith himself, The Lord said unto my Lord, Sit thou on my right hand, till I make thine enemies the footstool of thy feet." So again, before the Sanhedrin, the claim is made for Jesus, "Him did God exalt at his right hand, to be a Prince and a Savior" (5:31).

For the gift of the Holy Spirit, it is only necessary to remember the long quotation by Peter at Pentecost introduced by the words "but this is that which hath been spoken by the prophet Joel" (2:16-21). The return of Jesus to judgment is referred to as a fulfillment of prophecy by Peter when he speaks of Jesus "whom the heavens must receive until the times of restoration of all things, whereof God spake by the mouth of his holy prophets which have been since the world began" (3:21). Even the call to repentance is related to prophecy: "To him bear all the prophets witness, that through his name every one that believeth on him shall receive remission of sins" (10:43).

Of the fulfillment of prophecy in the witness to the gospel beyond the bounds of Israel we should not expect to hear in the earlier speeches in Acts, though the warnings of the rejection of the gospel by many in Israel are already sounded in Stephen's speech. But in the house of Cornelius, Peter, having said that "God is no respecter of persons, but in every nation he that feareth him and worketh righteousness is acceptable to him," concluded in the words quoted above (10:43) with the prophecy for "every one that believeth" in Jesus. At Antioch Paul repeats the claim that salvation is "for every one that believeth" (13:39), adding "Beware therefore lest that come upon you which is spoken by the prophets." James also at the Council of Jerusalem justifies the mission to Gentiles, saying that "to this agree the words of the prophets" (15:15). So in Paul's defense before Agrippa he includes among the things "the prophets and Moses did say should come" that Christ would "proclaim light both to the people and to the Gentiles" (26:22-23). And Paul's last words in Acts, before his Jewish hearers at Rome, are a declaration that as this people's heart is waxed gross, as the prophet Isaiah had said, so "this salvation of God is sent unto the Gentiles" (28:26-28).

Although in the epistles, written to converted Christians, we get only incidental references to the content of the gospel in its first proclamation, we get reminders of this note of fulfillment, whether it is by appeal to "the scriptures" in general (1 Cor 15:3, 4), to Abraham (Gal 3:6-8), to "the fathers" (Rom 15:8-12), or to the prophets (Rom 1:2; 3:21-22; 16:26; 1 Pet 1:10-12). It is an appeal with which the readers have been familiar from their first acquaintance with Christianity.

Fulfillment in the Third Gospel

The claim that Jesus was the Christ was in itself a claim that the Old Testament dispensation was fulfilled in the Christian faith. It is hardly surprising therefore that when Luke wrote his preface to the Gospel he should speak of "the things fulfilled" as its subject matter. Cadbury surely failed to appreciate the programmatic importance of the words when he wrote: "The suggestion that the fulfillment of Scripture is what Luke means need hardly be taken seriously, though of course πληρόω is so used."[5] Cadbury is nearer the truth in another, rather later, statement: "One feature of Luke's work that might be conscious intention, quite as well as traditional motif or subconscious conviction, is the evidence of divine guidance and control that pervades it. The divine intervention is one of the essentials of the Christian movement. Possibly this thought is already in his mind when he speaks of his subject as 'the things fulfilled among us'."[6]

Christianity was fulfillment, and the first Christians were bound to look to the Old Testament scriptures for illustrations of this. They could do so with varying degrees of insight, as is to be seen in the implications and the direct statements in all the Gospels. If, as I hold, Luke had Matthew before him, he had an abundance of instances available, including in all probability the formal quotations introduced by such words as "that it might be fulfilled." (That Mark was aware of at least one of them appears from his words in 4:12—"lest haply they should turn again and it should be forgiven them"—which reflect the quotation

---

[5]Henry J. Cadbury, "Commentary on the Preface of Luke," appendix C in pt. 1, vol. 2 of *The Beginnings of Christianity*, ed. F. J. Foakes Jackson and Kirsopp Lake (London: Macmillan, 1922) 496.

[6]*The Making of Luke-Acts* (New York: Macmillan, 1927) 303-304.

in Matt 13:15 of Isaiah 6:10.) But Luke does not use any of them, and only one (Matt 1:22) deals with a fundamental matter of Christology. These are at a comparatively superficial level, and the claim that Jesus fulfilled the old dispensation would be unaffected if none of them applied. Others are of a different kind: Matt 10:11 ("I send my messenger") is the traditional description of John the Baptist in Jesus' own words, so Luke copies this; three (Matt 26:4, 54, 56) speak of the necessity of the Passion, and Luke copies the first though he does not repeat the same message from the other two. To Luke, fulfillment is more than finding texts for details of Jesus' life; it is the fulfillment of the whole purpose of the Old Testament, behind which is "the determinate counsel and foreknowledge of God" (Acts 2:23); above all—as for Paul (1 Cor 15:3-4) so for Luke—it is the death and resurrection of Jesus that is "according to the scriptures."

In light of this analysis of the original kerygma as it appears in Acts, we can turn again to those elements in it that are covered in Luke's first volume.

The Davidic Origin. In Luke's introduction (chapters 1–3) he sets the scene for the whole Gospel. The immediate background of Jesus' mission was the mission of John the Baptist, and Luke therefore skillfully not only sets out the relation of Jesus to John, but deals completely with the story of John from the first promise of his birth until the time Herod "shut up John in prison." It is after this that the stage is cleared for the demonstration of Jesus' own work. The Baptist's mission was the immediate preparation for the gospel, appropriately therefore dealt with by Luke exclusively in this preparatory section, which in this and in broader ways puts the life of Jesus into its context.

Luke is concerned to show that Jesus' whole life was rooted in Israel. The Gospel begins in the temple where Zacharias, himself blameless in following the commandments and ordinances of the Lord, was fulfilling the prescribed rites. According to the precepts of the Law, Jesus was circumcised on the eighth day; he was presented in the temple "according to the law of Moses" (2:22). "Luke attaches great importance to this first coming of Jesus into the temple of Jerusalem, which is for him the center of the divine plan of salvation."[7] And when Jesus was twelve years old he was taken to Jerusalem for the Passover "according to custom" (2:42), regarding which Jeremias writes: "Incidentally the Talmud speaks of thirteen years as the borderline for the fulfillment of the Law. Luke 2:42 is not in contradiction with this rule; the twelve-year olds were brought on the pilgrimage in order to get them used to the event which would become a duty next year."[8] Jeremias's comment points to the accuracy with which Luke refers to local conditions (Luke has "according to custom" not

---

[7]Pierre Benoit and M.-É. Boismard, *Synopse des quatre Evangiles en français avec parallèles des apocryphes et des Pères,* 2 vols., revised and corrected by P. Sandevoir (Paris: Editions du Cerf, 1972; ¹1965–1977) 2:64.

[8]Joachim Jeremias, *Jerusalem in the Time of Jesus* (London; Philadelphia: Fortress, 1969) 76.

"according to the law"); and for Jesus these conditions are shown to be the loyalty of devout people to the law of Moses.

As Moses stood for the law so does Elijah for the prophets, and Luke in his introductory chapters sees the Baptist as the new Elijah "to turn the hearts of the fathers to the children, and the disobedient to walk in the wisdom of the just, to make ready for the Lord a people prepared for him" (1:17), to "go before the face of the Lord to make ready his ways" (1:76). We have the first indications of the interpretation "in all the scriptures" of the things concerning Jesus (24:27).

But above all Christianity claimed to be the fulfillment of the promises to Abraham and David. Throughout Luke's introduction is the theme of salvation coming to Israel, the sons of Abraham; so far there are no more than hints that the gospel is also to the Gentiles. There is no claim in these chapters that Abraham is to be "the father of many nations" (in the words cited in Rom 4:18) through the conversion of the Gentiles. Such a claim would have imported later theologizing into the contemporary scene. So the message to Zacharias tells him of what his son will do for "many of the children of Israel" (1:16); Mary is told that her son will reign "over the house of Jacob" (1:33), and in the Magnificat she speaks of God's help to "Israel his servant" and of his mercy "toward Abraham and his seed" (1:54-55). In the Benedictus, addressed to "the Lord, the God of Israel," Zacharias speaks of the salvation which God is bringing because of "his holy covenant, the oath which he sware unto Abraham our father" (1:72-73); and the angel's declaration to the shepherds is of good tidings "to all the people" (2:10)—the people, that is, of Israel. Those who welcomed the infant Jesus at his presentation have the same outlook: Simeon was "looking for the consolation of Israel" (2:25); and Anna gave thanks and spoke of Jesus "to all them that were looking for the redemption of Jerusalem" (2:38). The atmosphere throughout is purely Jewish, and although Simeon could speak of "revelation to the Gentiles" (2:32) and the Baptist say "God is able of these stones to raise up children unto Abraham" (3:8), these are but faint foreshadowings of what Luke is gradually to make plain. Like Matthew, Luke uses his genealogy (3:23-38), as he closes his introduction, to show Jesus as "the son of David, the son of Abraham" (Matt 1:1), though Luke closes with the words that are to reappear at crucial points in the Gospel—"the son of God" (3:38).

Redemption was awaited for God's people, but it was to be through the raising up of "a horn of salvation for us in the house of his servant David," as Zacharias expressed it (1:38-39). It is therefore important for Luke to stress that Jesus was in fact "the son of David." Mary is therefore introduced as "a virgin betrothed to a man whose name was Joseph, of the house of David" (1:27), through whom the genealogy of Jesus was to be traced. Mary herself was told that the Lord God would give her son "the throne of his father David" (1:32), and for his birth Joseph providentially took her "to the city of David, which is called Bethlehem, because he was of the house and lineage of David" (2:4). The significance of the birthplace was stressed again to the shepherds: "there is born to you this day in the city of David a Savior" (2:11).

That Jesus was in fact a "son of David" never seems to have been disputed, but there were no doubt many others who might make the same claim. That he was so did not prove his messiahship, but a denial of it would have been, at least in the eyes of many, in itself to invalidate such a claim. The title "son of David" is part of the earliest Christology; Paul could still refer to it in Rom 13 but the appeal of the phrase was greatest among the Jews. Other titles would begin to have more significance in the Gentile world, but this was an element of the most primitive preaching of the gospel. Luke gives it its due place. It is in illustrating the Davidic origin of Jesus that Luke makes use of the traditions he had received about the infancy of Jesus, and in the course of these speaks of the virginal conception. This is in no sense incidental, for clearly the gospel could not have been preached as demanding a prior acceptance of this as true. The descent of Jesus could not be challenged—hence its importance in the kerygma. But Luke, laying proportionately less emphasis than Matthew on Mary's virginity, records it as part of the tradition that he had received.

Luke has used his introduction to set out the claims that are to be justified in the rest of his work. In proclaiming Jesus as the Son of David he has indicated much more. Jesus, as Mary is told, is "the Son of the Most High" (1:32), "the Son of God" (1:35); God himself, as in Matthew, calls him "my beloved Son" (3:22). As Son of David he is "Christ the Lord" (2:11), or "the Lord's Christ" (2:26), and a king who was to receive "the throne of his father David" (1:32) and "reign over the house of Jacob for ever" and have a kingdom that would have no end (1:33). He is "a Savior" (2:11) through whom the salvation of God himself will be accomplished. So Zechariah can speak of the "horn of salvation" God has raised up (1:69) and of "the knowledge of salvation" now to come to God's people (1:77); and Simeon can rejoice that in Jesus he has "seen God's salvation" (2:30).

The salvation of God is to be for all mankind. The coming of Jesus is a "great joy which will come to all the poeple" of Israel (2:10), and it is first his people Israel that God, as Zechariah can say, has "visited and redeemed" (1:68), but Jesus is not only for glory to God's people Israel but also "a light for revelation to the Gentiles" (2:32). So the quotation from Isaiah ("the voice of one crying in the wilderness"), which Luke like Matthew uses, is extended to include the proclamation that "all flesh shall see the salvation of God" (3:6).

Finally, the opposition that Jesus and his disciples are to meet is already indicated: "This child is set for the fall and rising of many in Israel, and for a sign that is spoken against" (2:34). Luke has set out his claims for Jesus and his office: he is Christ, the Son of David, the Son of God, Lord and King, the Savior for all mankind. It will be for the rest of his work, in ordered development, to provide their justification.

The Ministry. There was bound to be a desire among those to whom the gospel was preached to know more about the life of Jesus and his public ministry, not only out of natural curiosity but also as witnessing to the claims made about him. To this was added the need to know what he taught, that he might be understood better, and for the guidance and encouragement of the converts in the situations in which they found themselves. Such information constitutes a large part of each of the Gospels, and their authors had therefore not only to collect or arrange such information, but also to select from available material what best served their purposes. That such selection was employed in John's Gospel is very obvious, as indeed it states (20:30; 21:25), but it must have been made in some measure by each of the evangelists. The discussions that have taken place about Luke's alleged "great omission" from Mark's Gospel have not always given sufficient weight to the need for such selection.

So far as Luke is concerned, it is obvious that he accepted Matthew as a reliable source, and that he had other sources he equally trusted. He did not live in a vacuum, and had every reason to know what was being taught in Christian churches. Out of all this, in the arrangement that best served his purpose, he made his selection. Indeed he indicates what it was both by the use he made of the narrative of Jesus' preaching at Nazareth (4:16ff.) and by the reply made to the messengers from the Baptist in prison (7:22). The claim made at Nazareth after the reading of the passage from Isaiah—"Today hath this scripture been fulfilled in your ears"—is implicit in the later episode also. The twofold program of Isaiah's words, the preaching of good tidings to the poor and the works of liberation and mercy, is made the theme of the Ministry. Both elements are already included in Matthew's Gospel, and when Luke makes omissions from it (as in parts of the Sermon on the Mount) he retains all he needs to build up his own structure.

So in setting out to show "all that Jesus began to do" Luke has one primary object: to show that Jesus was the Christ. He does it, not by using the title, which is kept back until the evidence that justifies it has been presented, but by recording the mighty works of Jesus in a continuous narrative, with repeated reminders that they raise the question of his person. Luke has therefore based his narrative on that of Matthew, limiting so far as is possible interrutions by lengthy discourses, and making such rearrangements as help build up his own structure. The gradual revelation of the meaning of Jesus' life that is made to the reader is in line with the revelation to the disciples: when Peter comes to his confession of Jesus as "the Christ of God" (9:20) the reader is expected to have come to the same conclusion.

The one apparent exception to this gradual development is in the words of demoniacs. The demonic powers recognize Jesus as their adversary and use titles (not however that of "the Christ") that show this. Already in the temptation story the devil uses the words "If thou art the Son of God," but this is when Jesus is without witnesses, and it reflects a truth that is in the consciousness of Jesus himself; Luke is of course keeping to the tradition, as in Matthew. Jesus is later addressed by demoniacs as "the Holy One of God" or "the Son of God," but on two of these occasions (4:34 and 4:41) Luke records the command of Jesus that they should be silent; there is no parallel here in Matthew. The third occasion is that of the Gerasene demoniac when Jesus is addressed as "the Son of the Most High God" (8:28); the events do not provide the opportunity for a similar rebuke, and silence is achieved by the banishment of the demons to the deep. But whatever the precise meaning of the addresses used by demoniacs, they stand apart from the general thrust of the narrative. It is not the words of demoniacs, but the acts of Jesus in exorcising them that contribute to the gradual development of Luke's theme.

"The works of the Christ" (to use the phrase of Matt 11:2) are portrayed from the first proclamation of the Nazareth sermon, throughout the continuing ministry in Galilee, and in the appeal made to their significance in reply to the question of the Baptist's messengers, on to the point where Peter makes his confession. Questions that intersperse the narrative repeatedly challenge the reader as to the meaning of the events related. Throughout the account of Jesus' doings the question lies in the background: "Who then is this?" It is raised in many forms. At Nazareth the question came in the simple form of wonder: "Is not this Joseph's son?" (4:22). At 4:36 (where there is no parallel in Matthew) the question in the synagogue becomes "What is this word? For with authority and power he commandeth the unclean spirits and they come out." At the healing of the paralytic, where Matt 9:3 has "This man blasphemes," Luke has the question: "Who is this that speaketh blasphemies? Who can forgive sins but God alone?" (5:21). On the lips of John's disciples there comes, as in Matthew, the direct challenge: "Art thou he that cometh" (7:20). In a Pharisee's house (again with no parallel in Matthew) men ask "Who then is this that even forgiveth sins?" (7:49); and after the stilling of the storm, where Matthew's question begins "What manner of man is this?" Luke has the more pointed question "Who then is this, that he commandeth even the winds and the water, and they obey him?" (8:25). At 9:9, where Matt 14:2 gives Herod's words as "This is John the Baptist," Luke again has a question: "Who is this, about whom I hear such things?" So at last Jesus asks his disciples, "Who do the multitudes say that I am?" (9:18, where Matt 16:13 has "Who do men say that the Son of man is?") and we come to the crucial question for Jesus' disciples—"But who say ye that I am?"—and Peter's answer on their behalf: "The Christ of God" (9:20). God's own witness follows in the Transfiguration: "This is my Son" (9:35); it is after that conclusion, with the exhortation "Hear ye him," that the Gospel goes on from 9:51 with its long exposition of Jesus' teaching.

Luke does not think in terms of proof that Jesus was the Christ, the Son of God; he things in terms of witness: the witness of the Father, at Jesus' Baptism and Transfiguration; the witness of the Scriptures, whose promises he fulfilled;

the witness of his own deeds and words; and, when Luke continues the story in Acts, the witness of those who had known him.

The Passion and the Resurrection. Already in treating the deeds of Jesus the narratives of Peter's confession and of the Transfiguration include references to the necessity of the Passion and Resurrection for the fulfillment of the divine purpose. In the former Jesus is recorded as saying that "the Son of man must suffer many things, and on the third day be raised up" (9:22). This is closely parallel with Matthew (16:21), except for two Lucan additions both followed by Mark: "and be rejected" is clearly a more accurate phrase to express the action of the elders, priests, and scribes, added for stylistic reasons; and Luke includes the phrase "the Son of man" as in the other predictions of the Passion (9:44; 18:31). It is only after the Resurrection that the form "the Christ should suffer" (24:26, 46) is used, as it is by Peter in Acts 3:18. It was then that the necessity of which Jesus spoke came to be clearly seen as the fulfillment of the prophets' "foreshadowing" of the Messiah (cf. 24:17, 46; Acts 3:18).

At the Transfiguration Luke alone relates that Moses and Elijah "spoke of his departure (ἔξοδος) that he was to accomplish (πληροῦν) at Jerusalem" (9:31). The word ἔξοδος as a word for death (ASV "decease"; ERV RSV NRSV NEB REB "departure") is normally followed by an explanatory phrase, such as "from life." In the New Testament it occurs again absolutely in 2 Pet 1:15, apparently with reminiscence of the Transfiguration (cf. 2 Pet 1:16ff.); in the Book of Wisdom it occurs twice, at 3:3 where "their departure" is parallel to "have died" in the previous half-verse and in 7:6 ("one entrance into life and a common departure") where "from life" is understood. The phrase in Luke is therefore remarkable, and with the word πληροῦν for "accomplish" or "fulfill" suggests and Old Testament analogy to the significance of Christ's death, resurrection, and ascension.

In passing to the next part of the Gospel (9:51ff.) Luke therefore has no need to stress fulfillment in the Ministry; he can look forward to fulfillment in the Passion, and his repeated notes that Jesus was on the way keeps Jerusalem always in mind as the goal (as Rome is in the latter part of Acts). So he begins with "When the days were being fulfilled for him to be received up." Only as Luke returns to Matthew's order at the close of this part of the Gospel does he include the third prediction of the Passion (18:31-34; Matt 20:17-19),[9] but the goal of Jerusalem is always in his thought.

The story of the Passion is told straightforwardly, as it was no doubt repeated in the churches, without interpretative comment, though its language is sometimes (as in Matthew) colored by that of the Old Testament; for instance, at 23:34-35 there are echoes of Psalm 22. At two points there are definite

---

[9]Matthew in all three predictions speaks of the Resurrection on "the third day"; Luke follows Matthew's usage; Mark on each occasion alters to "after three days."

references to fulfillment, both in passages peculiar to Luke and both on the lips of Jesus. At 22:22 Jesus is recorded as saying "For the Son of man indeed goeth, as it hath been determined," and at 22:37 "For I say unto you, that which is written must be fulfilled (τελεσθῆναι) in me. And he was reckoned with transgressors: for that which concerneth me hath fulfillment (τέλος ἔχει)."

We have already seen how the Passion and Resurrection are repeatedly interpreted in the last chapter of Luke. Christ's prediction "when he was yet in Galilee, saying that the Son of man must be delivered up into the hands of sinful men, and be crucified, and the third day rise again" is recalled (24:6-7). The necessity is related to "Moses and all the prophets" and "all the scriptures" (24:27), and again to "the law of Moses and the prophets and the psalms" (24:44).

The Ascension is in the Gospel related in few words and without comment, but it is significant that the traditional reference to Psalm 110 has already been made by Jesus before the Sanhedrin: "but from henceforth shall the Son of man be seated at the right hand of the power of God" (22:69).

Luke could hardly have described the matters of which he wrote better than by saying that they were "the things fulfilled among us."

Chapter 6

Tradition in the Gospel

Even as they delivered them unto us, who from the beginning were eyewitnesses and ministers of the word.   —Luke 1:2

The high authority that the written word of the New Testament has been
accorded in the subsequent history of the Church makes it difficult for Christians
of later generations to put themselves in the position of those for whom the test
of authenticity of doctrine was not to be found in books but in the unwritten
tradition (παράδοσις) of the apostles. Even in the latter part of the second
century, Irenaeus, who held the Gospels in honor, speaks of those "who in the
absence of paper and ink" are "barbarians, so far as regards our language," but
"have salvation written in their hearts by the Spirit without paper and ink,
carefully preserving the ancient tradition."[1] For Luke, whatever written sources
he may have had at his disposal, his trust in them had to depend on their
conformity with the apostolic witness, that is, with the tradition. He could trust
them precisely because they reported matters "even as they delivered
(παρέδοσαν) them unto us, who were from the beginning eyewitnesses and
ministers of the word." No such narratives had as yet received canonization from
the Church, but Luke lived in days when it was still possible to ascertain by
means other than a canon of New Testament scriptures what the apostolic
tradition meant. "The apostles' teaching" was indeed how he defined the content
of the faith of the first Christians (Acts 2:42).

The increase of literacy, and consequent dependence on the written word,
has taken away from the word "tradition" much of its implication of authority
and accuracy. To use it in the first century was to make a claim to both. "It is
often forgotten that it is tradition, not Scripture, which is, strictly speaking,
primary, and that among the criteria by which the claim of a particular document
was judged, was included that of conformity with a preexisting body of doctrine."[2] It is this criterion that Luke himself appeals to when he speaks of those
who wrote "even as they delivered" the facts, who "from the beginning were

---

[1]*Adv. haer.* 3.4.2.
[2]T. G. Jalland, *The Church and the Papacy* (London, 1944) 107.

eyewitnesses and ministers of the word." He had his own purpose in writing a new narrative, but the precise "even as" (καθώς) of Luke 1:2 is an indication that he used sources he judged trustworthy by this standard.

Tradition could be handed down orally or in writing, but the written word did not necessarily carry greater authority. When Irenaeus wrote "Against Heresies," he referred the heretics to "that tradition which originates from the apostles, which is preserved by means of the successions of presbyters in the churches";[3] it was within "the power of all, in every church, who may wish to see the truth, to contemplate the traditions of the apostles manifested throughout the whole world";[4] "the apostolic tradition has been preserved continuously."[5] The true tradition has been guarded as a deposit, lodged in the church, as a rich man deposits his money in a bank.[6] "Similarly," wrote R. O. P. Taylor, though apparently without this passage in mind, "Timothy is told (1 Tim 6:20) to guard the deposit—the figure being derived from a thing deposited in, say, a bank."[7]

Tradition, as the careful handing on of the truth, was highly valued. The Didache urges those to whom it is addressed to "hold fast to the traditions, neither adding nor subtracting anything" (Did 4:13). Nor was this care exercised only with regard to religious matters. Josephus speaks of events he had himself seen, and then later written down in "the tradition of the truth," a phrase that also occurs in Irenaeus.

The value of a tradition depended on the source from which it was drawn and the accuracy with which it was preserved. The traditions of the rabbis come in for criticism in the Gospels, but that does not throw any doubt upon their source, nor on the care with which they were preserved. Josephus could truly say that "the Pharisees have delivered to the people a great many observances by succession from their fathers."[8] It was not the process of transmission that was open to criticism.

Tradition is handing over. So Paul could say, "I received of the Lord that which I also delivered unto you" (1 Cor 11:23), and "I delivered unto you first of all that which I received" (1 Cor 15:3). Tradition was something received on authority, to be handed on to others, who should "hold the traditions" which they were taught (2 Thess 2:15). And the ultimate authority for Christians was that of those who "from the beginning were eyewitnesses and ministers of the word."

Clearly Luke was concerned that what he wrote should be part of the process of handing on the tradition. And to him one source for this—and indeed the only

---

[3]*Adv. haer.* 3.2.
[4]*Adv. haer.* 3.1.
[5]*Adv. haer.* 3.2.
[6]*Adv. haer.* 3.2.
[7]R. O. P. Taylor, *The Groundwork of the Gospels. With Some Collected Papers* (Oxford: Blackwell, 1946)_ 73; and see his chapter on "Tradition," 64-74.
[8]*Ant* 10.6.

extant source that we have—was Matthew's Gospel. The handing on of the tradition was a community activity, and we can see that Matthew's Gospel, whatever its ultimate origin, was to some extent a community product, with additions and revisions made at different times, until it took its final form. While we can accept that the text known to Luke was not yet completely in that form, there is good reason to believe that it was the earliest example of a written Gospel to be compiled. It is indeed remarkable that the earliest allusions to the Gospels' texts seem to be quotations from, or allusions to, Matthew. As I have pointed out in a previous book, this may well be so in the New Testament with the Epistle of James; it is so with the First Epistle of Clement, the letters of Ignatius, and the Didache.

The point was well made by Lagrange when he wrote:

> When one reflects that Clement wrote from Rome, where to all appearances the Gospel of Mark was born, and that Ignatius, in a Gentile milieu, should have had a preference for Luke, we can only explain that privileged position of Matthew by the start that he had over them. It was the first among the memoirs, and it kept its place as an echo of the Lord's words even after Luke had produced a large number of them.[9]

To the writer of the Didache, Matthew was *the* Gospel, and the source of many allusions. It is preeminently an ecclesiastical book, to be read in the Christian assemblies, and may have been, as has been often suggested, compiled for lectionary purposes. On the other hand, Luke's Gospel, while it was possible for it to be used in the liturgy, does not seen to have been so intended by its author. Luke's two volumes are written to be read through for the following out of a theme, not to provide lections for a calendar.

Farmer has suggested the possibility that when Luke spoke of "many who have taken in hand to compile a narrative"—the word "narrative" being in the singular—it was the Gospel of Matthew and the "many" who had a share in its development to which he was referring.[10] The suggestion raises the question whether the oft-quoted words of Papias, that "Matthew compiled the oracles in the Hebrew language, but everyone interpreted them as he was able,"[11] could refer to an early stage in its development. Whatever the history of Matthew's Gospel, it is clearly for Luke an authoritative work, written in accordance with the tradition received. When Luke rearranges or omits parts of Matthew, it is in

---

[9]Marie Joseph Lagrange, *Évangile selon saint Matthieu*, 7th ed. (Paris: J. Gabalda, 1948; [1]1923) ix, my translation, as quoted in *The Making of Mark. An Exploration* (Macon GA: Mercer University Press, 1989) 210.

[10]W. R. Farmer, *The Synoptic Problem: A Critical Analysis* (New York: Macmillan, 1964; rpt. with corrections, Dillsboro NC: Western North Carolina Press; Macon GA: Mercer University Press, 1976) 221.

[11]Eusebius, *Eccl. hist.* 3.9.16.

order to follow out his own plans; there is no reason to think that he questioned the reliability of Matthew's narrative.

For material Luke did not find in Matthew there may have been many sources, written or oral. After all he was writing from within the Christian Church, and was familiar with what was being taught. For the Infancy stories he seems to be making a claim to go back to the best informed source possible, when he writes "Mary kept all these things, pondering them in her heart" (2:10) and "his mother kept all these things in her heart" (2:51). Concerning the bulk of the Gospel the words of Dibelius are apposite: "In any case the frequent question whether an oral or a written tradition is to be accepted is a problem of secondary significance. A relative fixation which does not exclude variations is possible in the case of either the one or the other mode of handing down."[12] Oral tradition, especially of the words of Jesus, could be very conservative and Luke's text is sometimes more "primitive" than Matthew's.

The basic elements of the kerygma, as witnessed to by the early speeches in Acts, and for that matter by Rom 1:1-6, must from the first have been more fully explained and illustrated for the sake of Christian converts. Even in these speeches we have indications of details of the Gospels. This is so with the Ministry of Jesus: it began "from the baptism of John" (Acts 1:22); Jesus was "anointed with the Spirit and with power" (Acts 10:38); he was from Nazareth (2:22); and was attested by God "by mighty works and wonders and signs" (2:22); he "went about doing good, and healing all that were oppressed by the devil" (10:38); he preached throughout all Judea, beginning from Galilee" and in Jerusalem (10:37, 39). So with the Passion: he was crucified "by lawless men," that is, by Romans (1:23), after Pilate had "determined to release him" (3:13), because Jews had asked for "a murderer to be granted" in his place (3:14); Herod and Pilate had been "gathered together" against him (4:27); the witnesses to his resurrection had "eaten and drunk with him after he rose from the dead" (10:41).

Such details are only illustrations of what must have been inevitable in the preaching of the gospel. If Jesus went about doing good, Christians were bound to be given accounts of what this meant; if he did "mighty works and wonders and signs," they were bound to treasure the particular stories that justified the general statement. They were bound also to treasure the records of his sayings; not all of those then remembered have survived in our Gospels. According to Acts 20:35, Paul could tell his followers to "remember the words of the Lord Jesus," quoting words not included in any of the four Gospels, and which are doubtless not the only ones then remembered of which we have no record in the Gospels.

---

[12]Martin Dibelius, *From Tradition to Gospel*, trans. Bertram Lee Woolf (London: Robinson and Watson, 1934; New York: Charles Scribner's, 1965; Greenwood SC: Attic Press, 1982) 39.

The care with which traditions were handed down is illustrated occasionally by the incidental references to events that are not explained. We are not told how Pilate mingled the blood of the Galileans with their sacrifices, nor of the circumstances in which the tower in Siloam fell (Luke 13:1-5), but they were the occasion of sayings of Jesus which were remembered. It is the care for his words that has preserved the incidental historical reference. We have no record of mighty works done in Chorazin or Bethsaida, but the preservation of Jesus' words has resulted in their names going into the Gospel record (Matt 11:21; Luke 10:13). There is no reason to suppose any literery connection between the story in Luke 10:38-42 about the sisters Martha and Mary, and the references to them in John's Gospel, but the relations between the two sisters in Luke fits so naturally to that revealed in John that we can recognize we are in touch with carefully remembered events.

Between 4:1 and 9:50, Luke is clearly concerned to keep to Matthew's framework and, as far as this is apparent, to his chronology. The additions he makes to the text—the preaching at Nazareth, the miraculous drought of fishes, the widow's son at Nain, and the ministering woman (4:16-30; 5:1-11; 7:11-17; 8:1-3)—are inserted where Luke, having additional sources at his disposal, secures the least adjustment of Matthew'text. One exception is the story of the woman who was a sinner (7:36-50), which is not in any chronological framework, and, like the stories of the woman with a spirit of infirmity ("in one of their synagogues," 13:10-17) and of the man with the dropsy (in a Pharisee's house, 14:1-6) might equally well have been in the following section of the Gospel. None of these implies any particular chronology or locality; those that do—the ten lepers, Zacchaeus, the widow's mite—inevitably come at a later place.

Luke's non-Matthæan sources supply teaching material overlapping with Matthew's, some additional incidents, and a number of parables included in his teaching section. It is noticeable that his peculiar parables are in general of a different kind from Matthew's eschatological ones. They do not begin with "The kingdom of God is like" and the wider range is typical of Luke's interest, which as early as in the account of the Baptist's preaching was shown in his addition of the practical effects of penitence (3:10-14). Luke is concerned with didache as well as with kerygma, with the teaching that followed on for Christian converts after the first proclamation of the basic facts of the gospel. The teaching was the inevitable continuation of the preaching, and part of the process of handing on the tradition concerning Jesus.

According to Conzelmann, "whereas in Mark the narrative itself provides a broad unfolding of the kerygma, Luke defines the narrative as the historical foundation, which is added as a secondary factor to the kerygma, a knowledge of which is taken for granted."[13] In fact both Luke and Mark, and the latter in some respects more obviously (as in Mark 1:1-15), take a basic knowledge of the kerygma for granted. John does so more obviously than either. While Luke certainly has a keen sense of the historical, he is filling out the meaning of the kerygma, from the Davidic origin of Jesus to the Ascension.

To argue from the speeches in Acts to the Gospel of Luke might seem to be arguing in a circle since both come from the same pen. But the study of the Gospel itself shows how careful Luke is to hand on with the greatest accuracy what he has received. Dibelius cites two passages (Matt 11:2-6; Luke 7:18-23; and Matt 8:8-10; Luke 7:9), the record of the messengers of the Baptist and the story of the centurion at Capernaum, where Matthew and Luke vary greatly in the wording of the introduction and conclusion "but the kernel is handed down almost as a unity." The writers, Dibelius concludes, "clearly differentiated their responsibility towards the text of Jesus' words from their duties as narrators."[14] Dibelius does not envisage the possibility that Matthew is Luke's source, but that does not affect the point. Luke only makes small stylistic alterations when he copies the words of Jesus (or more strictly when he copies the Greek translation of them); he is freer when putting a narrative in his own way. Bultmann himself notes how Luke uses the phrase "it came to pass" (καὶ ἐγένετο) when he is not giving a definite context such as to "fit the course of events";[15] we have already seen how this is done when he varies from Matthew's order and does not wish to give a false chronological setting.

It would be surprising if Luke, so careful in the Gospel, were not careful also in Acts, though there he is concerned with giving summaries of speeches, and not with the preservation of words treasured as those of the Lord. It has often been asserted that, as ancient historians with their own outlook on the purpose of historical writing often invented suitable speeches to put into the mouths of those they wrote about, so Luke, as a historian, would feel as free to do so in Acts. The words of Thucydides are commonly quoted, as indeed they are by Cadbury: "Therefore the speeches are given in the language in which, as it seemed to me, the several speakers would express, on the subjects under consideration, the sentiments most befitting the occasion, though at the same time I have adhered as closely as possible to the general sense of what was actually said."[16] It is clear that Thucydides himself tried to get as near as he could to what had really been spoken. Not having access to original speeches, he did the best he could, and he warned his readers of his limitations. The case is quite

---

[13]Hans Conzelmann, *The Theology of St. Luke,* trans. Geoffrey Buswell (New York: Harper, 1961; Philadelphia: Fortress Press, 1982) 11.

[14]Dibelius, *From Tradition to Gospel,* 33, 34.

[15]Rudolf Bultmann, *The History of the Synoptic Tradition,* trans. John Marsh (Oxford: Blackwell; New York: Harper & Row, 1963) 360.

[16]Thucydides 1.22.

otherwise as concerns Luke. If, as we shall see, the traditional authorship of Acts is to be accepted, he was in a much better position to learn the facts; the content of the speeches was to him not a matter of mere interest, but of vital importance, and so far from warning his readers that he had had to use his imagination, he claimed to have "followed all things closely," so that his readers might know the certainty of the matters on which he wrote (Luke 1:3-4).

At this stage we are only concerned with the speeches in the first part of Acts; to those of Paul we shall return later. It is clear from the brevity of the speeches reported there that except in the case of Stephen's speech at his trial we are only given an outline of what must have taken much longer to deliver;[17] and their form is such that they are very different from the rhetorical exercises designed to add elegance to ancient histories.[18] They show every evidence of being faithful records of what was in fact said. That they are suitable to their particular occasions does not prove that they are just illustrations of Luke's artistic skill. A historian of World War II war wishing to include speeches by Churchill would not have to invent them to make them appropriate.

Stephen's speech (Acts 7:2-53) throws a valuable light not so much on Christian preaching as on Christian apologetic at a very early stage. He is defending himself at a time when Christians can still be regarded as a Jewish sect. The charge against Stephen is strictly a charge against an aberrant Jew: "This man ceaseth not to speak words against this holy place and the law: for we have heard him say that this Jesus of Nazareth shall destroy this place, and shall change the customs which Moses delivered unto us" (Acts 6:13-14). Stephen's offences are against the temple ("this holy place") and the law. His defence therefore is concerned with his teaching about Moses and about the temple. Specific Christian claims are, except at the end of the speech, implied rather than asserted. There are as it were Christian undertones in particular phrases, as when Moses is said to have been "mighty in his words and works" (Acts 7:22; cf. Luke 24:19); or in the statement that Moses was sent as "both a ruler and a deliverer" (Acts 7:35; cf. Acts 5:31). We come nearest to an explicit Christian pronouncement at Acts 7:37: "This is that Moses, which said unto the children of Israel, A prophet shall God raise up unto you from among your brethren, as he raised up me," a reference also cited by Peter in Solomon's Portico (Acts 3:22) and one which seems to have had its place in primitive Christian usage,[19] but one which became less significant when the Church moved out from its early Jewish environment. The logic of the speech is that God gave his promise to Abraham, which would be fulfilled when he should be served "in this place" (7:7); it was brought nearer to fulfilment when Moses came as a deliverer, but

---

[17]Cf. Dibelius, *From Tradition to Gospel*, 25.

[18]Cf. I. Howard Marshall, *Luke: Historian and Theologian* (Exeter: Paternoster Press, 1970; Grand Rapids MI: Zondervan, 1971) 56.

[19]Cf. C. H. Dodd, *According to the Scriptures* (London: Nisbet, 1952) 53-57.

he was even then misunderstood and opposed: "he supposed that his brethren understood how that God by his hand was giving them deliverance, but they understood not" (7:25). The Moses whom God chose as a ruler and deliverer was the Moses "whom they refused" (7:35), "to whom our fathers would not be obedient, but thrust him from them" (7:39). It is he who foretold that God would raise up a prophet like him (7:37). The tabernacle of Moses remained until David, who asked to "find a habitation for the God of Jacob" (7:46; cf. Ps 132). It was in fact Solomon who built a house, but "the Most High dwelleth not in houses made with hands" (7:48), as the prophet Isaiah had said. The people had always resisted the Holy Spirit; they had killed those who had shown them before "of the coming of the Righteous One" (7:51-52), in whom the house of David would be "made sure for ever" (2 Sam 7:16; cf. Luke 1:26).

The speech rings true to its context. The Jews had not understood Moses, they had not understood the significance of the temple, they had not now understood the Righteous One. It is the kind of speech Stephen could make; it is questionable whether it is the kind of speech Luke would have invented had he wanted to embellish his book with appropriate words of Christian witness.

I pass to the speeches of Peter. In general, like Stephen's, they give evidence of their primitive character, and in their content they give assurance of their substantial faithfulness to the earliest apostolic preaching. Negatively, there are no anachronistic elements that can be shown to have been imported into them from the more developed theology of a later period; positively, they reflect the conditions in which they are said to have been delivered.

On the day of Pentecost, Peter argues from the Old Testament to the truth of the outpouring of the Spirit, the Resurrection of Jesus, and his Ascension. The most developed theological conclusion drawn is that "God hath made him both Lord and Christ" (2:36). In the speech in Solomon's Portico, Peter appeals again to the Old Testament with the claim that Jesus was the prophet whom Moses had said God would raise up, and was God's servant. The implications of the identification of Jesus with the Servant of the Lord are indeed far reaching, but the speech does not draw them out; it is content with the statement that "the things which God foreshowed by the mouth of all his prophets, that his Christ should suffer, he thus fulfilled" (3:18). The statement does not go beyond what, for instance, is to be found in Luke 9:20-22, nor of course beyond the statements of Luke 24:26-27, 45-46. Before the Sanhedrin, recourse is made to the words of Psalm 118, that the stone set at nought "was made the head of the corner" (Acts 4:11); and on the second occasion, the claim is made that God exalted Jesus "at his right hand as Prince and Saviour" (5:31), an implicit appeal to Psalm 110. Finally, in the house of Cornelius, there is an exposition of Christian preaching to a group of Gentiles, who are assumed to have some knowledge of the gospel already (10:36). Jesus is described as anointed with the Holy Spirit, and ordained by God to be the judge of the living and the dead.

In all these speeches there is recourse to the Old Testament to vindicate the claims made about Jesus, and they are still of an undeveloped kind; Jesus as the prophet foretold by Moses, or the stone rejected by the builders, is proclaimed in terms that fade later into the background. Throughout, the stress is on the action of God, "the God of Abraham, Isaac, and Jacob," "the God of our fathers"; it was God who anointed Jesus, God who raised him, God who glorified him. All this has a genuine primitive ring, and Luke nowhere slipped into inserting ideas which could only have come from the later development of Christian theology. There is solid reason for regarding the speeches as fair statements of Peter's preaching. They give the tradition in the broadest outline; it is this which is filled in by Luke, primarily in the Gospel, and secondarily in Acts.

If Luke is justified in his claim to have investigated the course of events for a long time, it is understandable that he could have discovered enough about Peter's utterances to give summaries of their contents without being able to give the actual words of the speaker. With the speech of Stephen the case is different: it is reported at considerable length, and no attempt is made to reduce it to a mere summary. Moreover, it was delivered in circumstances when it was most unlikely that Christian hearers were present to remember what Stephen said. There was however one person who must have been present, who could follow the trend of Stephen's argument, and who must have brooded over it as he strove to resist its impact on him. The memory of the day when it was delivered was intensified by the sight of the faith and courage of the martyr's death, at which he was present and of which he approved. If the author of Acts was a companion of Paul, he had every opportunity of knowing what Paul remembered; he could have heard the story from Paul's own lips. It is time therefore to look into the question of the identity of the author of the Acts, and of the Third Gospel.

Chapter 7

The Author of the Gospel (I)

It seemed good to me also . . . to write.   —Luke 1:3

Was Luke "the beloved physician" and fellow worker of Paul the author of the Third Gospel and of Acts, as it was for many centuries believed, or are Luke and Acts from the pen of a later and therefore less authoritative witness to the events related? I propose in this chapter to set out the evidence for the traditional view, and in the next chapter to consider, within the limits possible, the objections that are alleged in disproof.

The Tradition

Whatever may be true of Matthew and Mark, Luke was certainly not published anonymously. No one writes to a named person, Theophilus, and says "it seemed good to me to write" without letting it be known who the writer is. Not unnaturally the "Muratorian Canon," one of the earliest witnesses to the tradition of Luke's authorship, says he wrote "in his own name" (*nomine suo*). But the obvious fact that the Gospel, like the Acts, is not an anonymous document is not always given the weight it deserves. Streeter has well commented on it:

> The other Gospels are anonymous; Luke is not. . . . Luke's preface would have no point at all if the original readers did not know the author's name. . . . It implies that the Church for which he wrote already possessed a work of the kind, but that he claimed to be in a position to improve upon it. But unless his name was well known—one might almost say unless he was known to have had some connection with the apostles—this claim would not have been admitted.[1]

More recently Dibelius has written:

> We must, of course, suppose that Luke's work before being accepted into the canon had a special literary title with the author's name in the possessive case.

---

[1]Burnett Hillman Streeter, *The Four Gospels. A Study of Origins, Treating of the Manuscript Tradition, Sources, Authorship, and Dates,* 4th impression revised (London: Macmillan, 1930; [1]1924) 558.

. . . Only when it was counted among the Gospels did Luke's book receive a title corresponding to that of the other Gospels.[2]

And Cadbury comments:

Where the title and author of a book were named on a separate tag, neither of these appeared on the inner text of the book.[3]

If Luke, Paul's companion, was not the author, it must have been at this stage that the actual author's real name was omitted and that of Luke substituted. It is an unlikely thing to have happened.

We have also to remember the tenacity of tradition in the ancient world, which was likely to have greater influence than any argument from the contents of the Gospel or Acts, for which indeed there is no evidence. In the case of the Second Gospel, Cadbury himself admits that "the name of Mark is not easily attributable to conjecture."[4] The same respect for tradition which could retain the name of Mark could also retain that of Luke. With his usual caution, Cadbury admits that it might really have been known in the second century, but adds: "but probably the tradition would have come into existence as early, and as definitely, if it were not known, on the basis above suggested"[5] (that is, on the internal evidence). It would not of course have been "quite as early" if the tradition was continuous from the time of publication, and there is no evidence that anyone found it necessary to prove Luke's authorship from the internal evidence of his writings.

It is tradition rather than deduction from the text of Luke-Acts that accounts for the earliest references to Luke as the author. The first of these may be the "Anti-Marcionite Prologues" to the Gospels. Their very existence witnesses to the acceptance of the fourfold Gospel, including that "according to Luke." It is significant that the biographical details included—that Luke was a Syrian of Antioch, that he was unmarried, and that he died in Boeotia—are not derived from the Gospel or Acts. At about the same time, Irenaeus wrote his book *Against Heresies* in which he insisted that there were, and could only be, *four* Gospels. His unhesitating assumption that Luke was the author of one of them implies that this was something long taken for granted, part of the tradition on which he so much relied, and something that would not be challenged by those against whom he wrote. For Irenaeus, two of the Gospels were written by apostles and two by their associates: Mark "the disciple and interpreter of Peter"

---

[2]Martin Dibelius, *From Tradition to Gospel,* trans. Bertram Lee Woolf (London: Robinson and Watson, 1934; New York: Charles Scribner's, 1965; Greenwood SC: Attic Press, 1982) 264n.2.

[3]Henry J. Cadbury, *The Making of Luke-Acts* (London/New York: Macmillan, 1927) 195.

[4]Ibid., 66.

[5]Ibid., 356.

and Luke "the companion of Paul."[6] It is the most natural conclusion that the same meaning lies behind the words of Justin who quotes freely from Matthew and Luke when he speaks of memoirs written "by apostles and those who followed them."[7]

There is no reason to suppose that Irenaeus arrived at his conclusion from the contents of any of the four Gospels; with Matthew and Mark it would have been an impossible task. Indeed in a book where so much stress is laid upon the importance of traditions and of its being open to all it would be surprising if his belief as to the authorship of any of the Gospels had any other basis than that he had received it as accepted tradition from an earlier age.

Finally, from the same period there is the witness of the "Muratorian Canon" that the "third book of the Gospels according to Luke" was written by the physician who had been a companion of Paul.

There can be no doubt that as far as the evidence of tradition is concerned, it is strongly in support of the authorship of Luke, Paul's fellow worker.

The "We-Sections"

The first person, which was used in Luke 1:3 and Acts 1:1, reappears in Acts in the so-called "we-sections" (16:10-17; 20:5-15; 21:1-18; 27:1–28:16). Either these sections constitute a claim by the author of having been present on the occasions to which they refer, or some other explanation is needed why this form is used. Irenaeus had already noticed this, but there is nothing to suggest he argued from them to the Lucan authorship, on which he had no doubts.

On linguistic grounds it is certain that in their existing form the "we-sections" come from the same hand as the rest of Acts. William Ramsay in commenting on this was moved to the rather acid words:

> This argument is absolutely conclusive to every person that has the power of comprehending and appreciating style and literary art; unfortunately many of the so-called "Higher Critics" seem to have become devoid of any such comprehension through fixing persistently their attention on words and details.[8]

Attention to words and details, however, has itself shown that either the author of Acts is the person whose presence justifies the change from "they" to "we" when speaking of Paul's companions, or if he used someone else's record he revised and rewrote it in his own style with the greatest consistency. We have already seen how carefully he avoided giving false impressions when, though recording the words of Matthew's Gospel, he changed the order in which some

---

[6]*Adv. haer.* 3.1.1.

[7]*Dialogue* 103.19.

[8]William Mitchell Ramsay, *Luke the Physician, and Other Studies in the History of Religion* (London: Hodder & Stoughton, 1908; rpt. Minneapolis: James Family, 1978) 34.

episode was related. It is incredible that he could fail to see that "we" gave the impression of the writer's presence, and equally incredible in view of the way in which he has consistently written that he should be deliberately misleading. The summary of Arnold Ehrhardt, cited without comment by C. K. Barrett, is justified:

> This leaves the reader with a plain choice; he may either accept the suggestion, made by the book itself, as true, or reject it, preferring the view that the book is a forgery.

Barrett only adds: "Ehrhardt insists upon this word."[9]

The "we-sections" are clearly meant to imply the presence of one of Paul's companions. Of the possible companions, some are excluded by the reference to them in Acts, some because they are known to have joined him too late to qualify. Two persons are possible: Titus and Luke. Neither of them is mentioned by name in Acts, and the suggestion that both names refer to the same person is excluded by 2 Tim 4:10. Of the two possible companions, there is no reason for preferring Titus to Luke, in face of the unanimous tradition that the author was Luke. Moreover, if, as I believe, the suggestion is well grounded that the author of Acts was Paul's amanuensis in writing the Pastoral Epistles, which include one to Titus, that would rule Titus out any way.

In his commentary on Acts, Haenchen, who assumes a late date for it (for him "the Temple had long lain in ruins when Luke wrote Acts") and therefore rejects the traditional authorship, questions the significance of the "we-sections." He asks how the readers would have understood the first introduction of the word "we." A group of three—Paul, Silas, and Timothy—had so far been mentioned. "That other persons had joined this group of three," Haenchen observes, "is nowhere stated or even indicated." So he concludes: "If now the narrative suddenly employs the first person plural, then the ancient reader would naturally have thought: Here one of these three men is introduced in the 'we' style."[10] Haenchen therefore asks:

> What did the ancient reader understand by the "we"? Did it suggest to him that an eyewitness is speaking, or did it suggest an eyewitness was the author of the work? Or finally, was it possible for such a reader to have considered the "we" as merely a stylistic device to bring the reader into closer touch with the events related?[11]

---

[9]C. K. Barrett, *Luke the Historian in Recent Study* (London: Epworth, 1961) 52.

[10]Ernst Haenchen, *The Acts of the Apostles: A Commentary*, trans. Bernard Noble and Gerald Shinn with Hugh Anderson and R. McL. Wilson (Oxford: Basil Blackwell; Philadelphia: Westminster, 1971) 630.

[11]Ibid., 490-91.

What the ancient reader, as represented by Irenaeus and those in the tradition behind him, not only must have understood but in fact did understand was not only that "we" was meant to include an eyewitness, but that it also included the "I" of Acts 1:1 and the "me" of Luke 1:3, and that this was in fact Luke the beloved physician. There is no problem if they came to the book as known to be Luke's and did not have to begin with the internal evidence.

The "stylistic device" theory is just not good enough. Haenchen himself seems to have modified its claims, since he later wrote:

> Martin Dibelius, to whom we are so greatly indebted for a new understanding of Acts, probably saw the matter correctly: Luke's "we" is a literary form! But what does that mean? Dibelius offers two possibilities: the "we" may suggest that the narrator himself took part in the journey; or it may mean that for some of the trips he was able to depend upon reports from an eyewitness. I consider the latter possibility the correct explanation.[12]

What it does not explain is how Luke, so carefully revising someone else's writing, was so careless, or so perverse, as to leave this glaring inconsistency.

On the face of it Luke tells a consistent story; the "we-sections" begin at Troas, at which point the author says "we sought to go into Macedonia." The narrative continues as far as to Philippi, but when the time for departure came it was Paul and Silas ("they") who left. Then at 20:5 Paul and his companions were back at Troas, where "*they* were waiting for *us*," and so "*we* sailed away from Philippi" and rejoined them. Then "we" travelled to Miletus, and then on to Jerusalem. When the time came for Paul to be sent to Rome, "it was decided that we should sail for Italy," and this last "we-section" continues until it is reached.

We get a wrong picture, however, if we think of Acts as being a book that has four special sections to be explained. It can perhaps best be put by saying that if we are to talk of "we-sections" we ought also to talk of "they-sections." In each case the words refer to Paul's companions, and, while "they" are spoken of until the first arrival at Troas (16:8) and again after Paul left Philippi (17:1) when "they" means Paul and Silas (and, as appears later, Timothy) until their return to Troas (20:4), the word "they" does not reappear for Paul's companions for the rest of Acts. That is to say, if we are to separate "we" and "they" sections, "they" is appropriate until 16:10; "we" becomes appropriate from 16:10 to 39; "they" is again necessary for 16:40–20:4); but "we" for the rest of the book. After the first use of "we" there is only one interruption when "they" becomes necessary, and that in the interval between Paul's leaving Philippi and

---

[12]Haenchen, "The Book of Acts as Source Material for the History of Early Christianity," in *Studies in Luke-Acts: Essays Presented in Honor of Paul Schubert*, ed. Leander E. Keck and J. Louis Martyn (Nashville: Abingdon, 1966; Philadelphia: Fortress Press, 1980) 272.

his return to it (16:40–20:4). Passages that deal with speeches or Paul's arrests do not involve references to his companions, and "we" continues to be the word in the background. From 16:8 onwards, all references to Paul's entourage are in the first person, with the exception of one interval, accounted for if the member of it keeping the record was left for the time at Philippi.

Two things emerge: first, the narrative is then completely straightforward. It is understandable that the writer deals with events at Philippi at great length as he might well do if he were present; and that when Paul and Silas move on he speaks very shortly of what happened as they passed through Amphipolis and Apollonia, to Thessalonica and Beroea, and so to Athens. Even at Athens, apart from the inclusion of Paul's speech, there is only the briefest of biographical information. Luke's concern is with the extension of the gospel rather than with the details of Paul's career. For that reason, when Paul had earlier revisited Phrygia and Galatia where he had already preached, Acts rapidly summarizes the voyage (16:4-8); after Paul had left Corinth, there is the same rapid summary of his passage to Caesarea and Antioch (18:18-22), and again "from place to place through the region of Galatia and Phrygia" (18:23). It is only when he went to the great center Ephesus, where he was breaking new ground, that the events are treated at greater length. After that there is again the briefest statement (20:1-5) until the arrival at Troas where "we" joined him. After that, and for the rest of the book, the author is in close touch with all that is happening, and reports events sometimes even from day to day.

There is a second consideration. The record with Paul's companions being referred to in the first person is only interrupted once, between his two moves from Troas to Philippi and from Philippi to Troas. If there is a problem, it is not with the "we" narrative but with the "they" section. If the use of "we" were only a stylistic device, there would be no good reason why it should not have been continued to be used throughout: "Now when we had passed through Amphipolis and Apollonia, we came to Thessalonica." The two points of contact at Philippi constitute too much of a coincidence to be convincing, unless Luke was in fact left at Philippi for the intervening period. Otherwise, with the use of "we" as merely a stylistic device, it is difficult to see how the ancient reader—especially one to whom in Haenchen's words "reflectiveness and literary sophistication were foreign"[13]—would have distinguished this from a pious fraud.

Incidentally, if Luke was left at Philippi for the period covered in Acts between 17:1 and 20:5, there may be a personal interest reflected in the special, almost proud way in which the city of Philippi is introduced (Acts 16:12). There is some doubt about the exact text, usually translated as "Philippi, which is the leading city of the district of Macedonia, and a Roman colony," but perhaps better understood as "Philippi, which is a city of the first district of Macedonia,

---

[13]Haenchen, *Acts of the Apostles,* 67-85.

and a Roman colony." In either case the phrase speaks of the dignity of the city, in terms that have no parallel in the introduction in Acts of the names of any other cities. Luke's acquaintance with it is confirmed by the detail of Acts 16:13—"outside the gate, to the riverside, where we supposed there was a place of prayer"—and by the reference to Lydia. One may wonder whether the "most excellent Theophilus," addressed at the beginning of both Luke and Acts, may have been stationed in this Roman colony where Luke could have become well acquainted with him. The unique formality of the address to Theophilus, and the unique formality of the reference to the city of Philippi may reflect such a connection. One can only speculate, but it would then have been very appropriate for Luke to have dedicated his books to such a person.

If the case put forward by J. A. T. Robinson in his *Redating of the New Testament* is valid, and the Pastoral Epistles were written during the years 57 and 58, there is confirmation of the reliability of Acts into which they can be fitted, and there may well be strong support for the authorship of Acts by Luke. "Only Luke is with me" (2 Tim 4:11) falls into line with the "we-sections" of Acts. As to the Pastorals themselves, a strong case can be made out that they came from Paul, but that Luke himself was the writer at Paul's dictation. In his commentary on the Pastoral Epistles, Lock noted that it is a natural suggestion from 2 Tim 4:11 "that St Luke was the amanuensis of 2 Tim., and there is a considerable quantity of Lucan non-Pauline words in all these Epistles." But he added, "I doubt whether St Paul would have allowed such freedom to an amanuensis."[14] At a later date, however, J. N. D. Kelly writes that

> the common assumption almost always is that the apostle dictated his letters in the word-for-word fashion conventional today. Modern research, however, has rendered this extremely doubtful. There is reason to suppose that, again because of the materials available, dictation was a much slower, more laborious process than it is nowadays, and that it was therefore necessary, instead of dictating word by word, to allow a trusted amanuensis a much freer hand in the composition of a letter.[15]

It is clear that all three Pastoral Epistles are stylistically the same, and that therefore the same hand wrote them. The strong Lucan character of the language used in them has been long recognized. Lock himself quoted several from Holtzmann's list of thirty-four "Lucan non-Pauline words"; a further list is given in

---

[14]Walter Lock, *A Critical and Exegetical Commentary on the Pastoral Epistles,* ICC (Edinburgh and New York: T. & T. Clark, 1924) xxix.

[15]J. N. D. Kelly, *The Pastoral Epistles. 1 Timothy, 2 Timothy, Titus,* Black's N.T. Commentaries; Harper's N.T. Commentaries (London: Adam & Charles Black, 1963; New York: Harper & Row, 1964) 26.

excursus 2 in C. F. D. Moule's *The Birth of the New Testament*,[16] and these are far from exhaustive. In a more extended study, not only of words, S. G. Wilson[17] has shown the strength of the case for Luke's hand in the Pastorals, though without examining the case also for this being done on Paul's behalf. It would carry us beyond our present study to pursue this further, but the evidence is in favor of the actual writing of the Pastorals by the hand of Luke, acting as Paul's "personal assistant," and incidentally for the traditional authorship of Luke-Acts. And as one of the Pastorals is addressed to Titus, this would mean the elimination of his name as the companion implied by the "we-sections" of Acts.

Medical Language as Evidence

It is well known that W. K. Hobart in his *The Medical Language of St Luke*[18] came to the conclusion that there was "a prevailing tinge of medical diction" in Luke-Acts which proved the author to be a doctor. Since the examination of this by Cadbury, it is no longer possible to say that this has been proved. It is however fair to Hobart to add that he did not suppose every one of the phrases he cited provided an equally cogent argument. What remains, however, is that the language of the Gospel and Acts is such as to confirm rather than to contravene the authorship by a medical man. Haenchen is overcaustic when he speaks of "the myth of Luke's medical language."[19] Even in a modern book the use of words like "syndrome," or "cerebral," or "complexes"—all medical terms—would not prove the writer to be doctor, and it is only in a very limited degree that the language of an ancient author writing on medical themes would be particularly technical, or distinct from that of any educated writer. What is more significant than medical language is medical interest. In a few cases (e.g., Luke 4:38; 5:12; 8:44) Luke seems to use phrases that are distinctive of or more natural to medical authors; and when, as in the references given, Luke is, as I hold, rewriting episodes from Matthew, there is more significance to be attached to the phrases he uses.

In Acts 28:8ff., where it is said that "the father of Publius lay sick with the fever and dysentery" (one of the more persuasive uses of medical language) and that he was cured (ἰάσατο) by Paul, the narrative continues: "And when this had taken place, the rest of the people of the island who had diseases also came and

---

[16]Charles F. D. Moule, *The Birth of the New Testament* (London: Black; New York: Harper & Row, 1962) 220-21.

[17]Stephen G. Wilson, *Luke and the Pastoral Epistles* (London: S.P.C.K., 1979).

[18]W. K. Hobart, *The Medical Language of St. Luke: A Proof from Internal Evidence That "the Gospel according to St. Luke" and "the Acts of the Apostles" Were Written by the Same Person, and That the Writer Was a Medical Man* (Dublin: Hodges, Figgis; London: Longmans, Green, 1882).

[19]Haenchen, *The Acts of the Apostles*, 43.

were healed (ἐθεραπεύοντο; ERV and RSV "cured"). The distinction between the word "cured" in the case of the father of Publius and that used for the others who had diseases may be purely linguistic, but it may point to the medical care of the latter, since the word θεραπεύω means in the first place "to attend on" (as in Acts 17:25) and derivatively "to tend," and only by a further extension "to heal." It may therefore well be that Luke (included among those to whom many gifts were later presented) gave ordinary medical attention, though prayer and the laying on of hands would not be excluded. In Luke 9:11, where Matthew has the word I have translated "heal" as equivalent to "cure" ("he healed their sick," ἐθεράπευσεν τοὺς ἀρρώστους αὐτῶν), Luke has "he cured those who had need of treatment" (τοὺς χρείαν ἔχοντας θεραπείας ἰάτο), which also suggests a professional attitude.

There is a further, rather intriguing consideration. If, as has been suggested, Luke was Paul's amanuensis for the Pastorals, there may be now light on 1 Tim 5:23: "Be no longer a drinker of water, but use a little wine for thy stomach's sake and thine often infirmities." It seems, says Kelly, "at first sight to interrupt the connection between 22 and 24ff., and critics have often assumed either that it has got misplaced or that it is a gloss which has crept into the text."[20] It is a pleasant, and a quite serious question to ask whether we have here one simple prescription of the "beloved physician" included as he relayed Paul's messages.

While the evidence of medical usage cannot be conclusive, it certainly gives a measure of support for the attribution of authorship to Luke the physician. It is consistent with the evidence on other grounds, and that is itself very strong.

---

[20]Kelly, *The Pastoral Epistles,* in loc.

Chapter 8

The Author of the Gospel (II)

It seemed good to me also . . . to write.   —Luke 1:3

That Paul's fellow worker Luke was the author of the Third Gospel and Acts is supported by objective evidence: the consistent tradition of early writers; the use of the first-person plural in Acts, which taken in its most natural sense limits the candidates for authorship to two, of whom Luke is the obvious choice; the accurate knowledge the author of Acts shows in referring to details of local administration as it was at the time of the events recorded, and to the persons in high office, and to local conditions in different places, all of which speaks of a contemporary acquaintance with the facts. Most English scholars seem to have been convinced by such evidence. On the other hand, it has been argued on other grounds, notably among German scholars, that Luke could not have been the author, and this is assumed rather than argued in a number of recent Lucan studies.

With the question of authorship two other questions are involved: the date and the historical value of Acts. A very late date in the first century or a second century date would itself rule out Luke's authorship, but it is the judgment on authorship that will suggest the date rather than that a knowledge of the date will settle the question of authorship. As to historicity, a distinction has to be made. If Luke was indeed the author, that would not rule out the possibility of some errors of fact; and with such errors, which are sometimes alleged, we are not therefore concerned in studying the question of authorship. For part of Acts recourse must have been made to sources accepted as trustworthy by the author; there is nothing to suggest they were sources Luke could not have accepted. On the other hand, a proof of fundamental discrepancy between the known facts and the statements of Acts would certainly rule out the traditional authorship.

If the argument developed in this book is valid, it follows that the Third Gospel, closing with the formal "dismissal" of the Ascension so as to lead on to the beginning of the second volume, was written before Acts; and that therefore the earliest date possible for the publication of the two-volume work must be at the end of Paul's two-year imprisonment in Rome; that means the early years of the seventh decade A.D. The terminus a quo can no longer be put at A.D. 70 on the ground that Luke shows knowledge of the fall of Jerusalem in that year, which has been shown to be baseless, notably recently by J. A. T. Robinson in his *Redating the New Testament*; such knowledge would not have been inconsistent with Luke's authorship, but the point has ceased to be important. The same is true of the claim that Acts shows dependence on Josephus's *Antiquities*; if this had been true, it would still have been possible to defend Luke's authorship, though it would have meant a date in his extreme old age; according to the "Anti-Marcionite Prologue" Luke lived to be eighty-four. But the claim that the author of Acts used Josephus cannot be substantiated, and seems now to be generally abandoned.[1]

The most serious objection to the authorship of Acts (and therefore of the Gospel also) by Paul's fellow worker Luke is made on the ground that the account of Paul's career in Acts is inconsistent with statements by Paul in his letters, which must constitute the primary authority; and that the theology of the speeches attributed to Paul in Acts is inconsistent with that of his letters, showing that the author of Acts could not have been close to him.

First of all, there are events in Paul's career that in Acts are passed over in silence. Paul's visit to Arabia after his conversion (Gal 1:17) is not referred to in Acts 9; the sufferings Paul refers to in his letters to the Corinthians (1 Cor 4:9-13; 15:32; 2 Cor 1:8; 4:8-12)—"the affliction that befell him in Asia," his fighting "with beasts at Ephesus," and whatever else Paul referred to—are not mentioned by Luke; neither for that matter are many of the sufferings of his life that Paul recounts when he is reduced to speak "as in foolishness, in this confidence of boasting" (2 Cor 11:16-32). If the purpose of Luke had been to write a life of Paul, these would indeed be serious omissions. Paul is sometimes referred to as Luke's hero, but if the word "hero" is used for the central character of a narrative, it has to be remembered that the "hero" of Acts is not Paul but the gospel. The conventional title "the Acts of the Apostles" is liable to mislead us, with its suggestion of a biographical purpose. The real theme of Acts is the proclamation of the kerygma: first the Ascension and the Gift of the Holy Spirit, and then the Apostolic Witness, from Jerusalem to the ends of the earth, with its message of Judgment and call to Repentance. The Gospel was no doubt spreading in other directions than the West—it was known in Alexandria for example—but providence had thrown Luke in with Paul, and no better illustration of the Apostolic Witness could be given than that which led to Rome, the capital of Luke's world.

If the argument already developed in this book is sound, the Third Gospel shows its author to be a person with care about accuracy, but also capable of selectivity in choosing what fell in with his objective. His omissions are wholly in accord with his method.

---

[1]Cf. C. S. C. Williams, *The Acts of the Apostles,* Black's N.T. Commentaries; Harper's N.T. Commentaries (London: Adam & Charles Black; New York: Harper & Row, 1964) 19ff.

Similar considerations apply to the absence of references to Paul's letters or indebtedness to their contents. If Luke was not writing a "Life of Paul," even less was he writing his "Life and Letters." A later writer about Paul would certainly have to refer to Paul's letters for information and to deal with the occasions of their being written. It is precisely during the period when they had not been collected together, and when, as far as much in them is concerned, they could still be thought of as dealing with particular and occasional needs, that the story of Acts could proceed without reference to their existence and without their being consulted as a source of biographical information. To the question of the substance of the speeches in Acts and of the epistles we shall have to return; but so far as biographical information is concerned, the fact that the narrative in Acts has not been fashioned to dovetail neatly into references in the epistles is a strong argument for the kind of date consistent with Luke's authorship.

There is at least an apparent contradiction between what Acts says about the movements of Silas and Timothy from the point when Paul left Thessalonica for Athens and Corinth (Acts 17:10–18:5), and what Paul himself says in 1 Thessalonians (3:1-6). According to Acts, Paul and Silas were sent from Thessalonica to Beroea, then Paul was sent on to Athens, Silas and Timothy staying at Beroea, and Paul waited for them at Athens; from there Paul went to Corinth and Silas and Timothy came down from Macedonia to join him there. According to 1 Thessalonians, at Athens Paul sent Timothy to Thessalonica; Timothy later rejoined him. The two accounts are not necessarily inconsistent. To Luke, the visit of Timothy back into Thessalonica was irrelevant if he himself was at this time (in a "they-section") left at Philippi; only the broad outline of Paul's advance mattered to Luke; after Paul had waited for his friends at Athens (where according to 1 Thessalonians Timothy at least joined him), he had gone on to Corinth, and Luke knew that Silas and Timothy were with him there. Granted Luke's particular interests and his being away at Philippi at the time, he can be seen to give a broad picture of the missionaries' movements. What at any rate is clear is that even if the information in Acts is inaccurate the inaccuracy is such that it could still be that of Luke, Paul's colleague.

A more intractable problem is that of the relation of the account of the Council in Acts 15 to the statements of Paul in Galatians 2. A number of solutions have been canvassed,[2] the two most widely held being that (1) the visit mentioned in Galatians 2 is the same as that of Acts 15 and that (2) it is the same as that of Acts 11. The former still seems the most probable. It was the view of Lightfoot that this is shown by a noteworthy series of correspondences: "The *geography* is the same. . . . The *time* is the same, or at least not inconsistent. . . . The *persons* are the same. . . . The *subject of dispute* is the

---

[2]For a summary of these, see Williams, *The Acts of the Apostles,* 24-30; see also J. A. T. Robinson, *Redating the New Testament* (London: SCM Press; Philadelphia: Westminster, 1976) 38-42.

same. . . . The *character of the conference* is the same. . . . The *result* is the same."[3] This is strong confirmation.

Alternatively, it has been held that the visit of Galatians 2 is that recorded in Acts 11, on the ground that otherwise Paul must have passed this visit over in silence, as he has indeed done with the decrees of the Council in epistles that must certainly have been written later. But the visit of Acts 11 was not to the apostles, and could well have been regarded by Paul as a piece of irrelevant information. It is surely not surprising that with the kind of documents at our disposal, we cannot neatly dovetail everything together. Luke is likely to have had available three different sources of information for what he relates in Acts 11–15: one dealing with Paul's Mission, 11:19-30, 12:25–14:28; one dealing with Peter, 12:1-24; and one with the account of the Council, 15:1-35. (Perhaps the division between chapters 14 and 15 should be between 15:2 and 15:3, but this does not materially change the situation.) What is relevant to our present concern is not the precise history, but the fact that there is nothing that invalidates the possibility of Luke being the editor.

That some authoritative decree of the Church was made, such as we find in Acts 15:28-29, seems to be confirmed by Rev 2:20 and 2:24; and unless some such decision was made, there is no indication why the Judaizing activities of Paul's opponents ceased as they did. Paul's own influence might have prevailed in the churches of his own foundation, but would hardly have settled the matter in Jerusalem itself. In Acts 15:3 we are told that when Paul and Barnabas were on their way to Jerusalem and passed through Phoenicia and Samaria, "they caused great joy unto all the brethren." But when they arrived at Jerusalem, which must still have retained some store of goodwill for Barnabas for his past benefaction, it is stated more cautiously that "they were received ($\pi\alpha\rho\epsilon\delta\acute{\epsilon}\chi\theta\eta\sigma\alpha\nu$; RSV "welcomed") of the church and the apostles and the elders," but that "certain of the sect of the Pharisees who believed" rose up in criticism of them (15:4-5). In contrast with this, the subsequent visit of 21:17ff. is recorded with the words "When we were come to Jerusalem, the brethren received us gladly." To account for the change something like the events of Acts 15 must be assumed.

According to Acts, the Council opened with "much debate" (15:7 RSV); the author does not regard it as advancing his general purpose to give particulars. He may well have thought that at the time of writing much of what had been said could well be forgotten; he is even more likely to have thought that it had ceased to be relevant to his readers. Whatever passions may have been aroused, that part of the proceedings closed when Peter made his speech bearing witness to what God had revealed to him on the issue. After this, "all the multitude kept silence, and they hearkened unto Barnabas and Paul" (15:12). It looks as if this was the

---

[3]J. B. Lightfoot, *St Paul's Epistle to the Galatians* (London: Macmillan, 1865; [10]1890; rpt. Grand Rapids MI: Zondervan, 1953) 123-24.

first moment that they could get the hearing they needed. It is significant that their names occur in that order; they had before in Acts become "Paul and Barnabas" or even "Paul and his company" (13:13). It is presumably meant to imply that Barnabas and Paul spoke in that order; and the sequence Peter, Barnabas, and Paul was psychologically sound.

The account of the Council, however selective the author may have been with his material in accordance with the main purpose of his book, does correspond to a real historical situation. He certainly regularly selects from the available material those things that most readily illustrate his theme, the carrying of the witness into the Gentile world. In 2 Cor 11:26-27, Paul himself lifts the curtain a little on many of the troubles he had in this process; it is almost accidentally that he reveals how many they had been. Luke speaks specifically of two of them (the stoning at Lystra and the beating at Philippi), and refers to other disorders such as the uproar at Thessalonica (17:5) and "the stirring up and troubling of the multitudes" at Beroea (17:13), but does not let such events deflect him from his main purpose. The goal of the narrative is not the martyrdom of Peter or Paul, but "preaching the kingdom of God and teaching about the Lord Jesus Christ" being given in Rome "openly and unhindered" (28:31 RSV).[4] Differences of treatment between the writings of Luke and Paul do not make it necessary to deny Luke's authorship of Acts. Both select those items of information that are significant in the development of their themes. Their purposes, though consistent with each other, are different; and it is not surprising that there are gaps in the links between them.

There are other historical facts alleged in Acts that have been called in question by various writers, and there are those who do not flinch from speaking of many of its contents as fiction. Goodenough, for example, questions whether Paul was in fact a Roman citizen: "Paul the Roman citizen seems to me in all probability still another part of Luke's fiction."[5] Goodenough cites Paul's own words that he had been beaten three times with rods by the Romans, and adds "but from that we are probably to deduce that he failed to stop the torture by announcing that he was a citizen because in point of fact, he was not."[6] Acts itself records one such beating (16:23), and if there were two more we do not know the circumstances; Paul does not in fact say that they were "by the Romans," though beating with rods was the Roman manner. But Goodenough is not afraid to draw the conclusion from his thesis:

---

[4]Henry J. Cadbury, *The Making of Luke-Acts* (London/New York: Macmillan, 1927) 320, 323.

[5]Erwin R. Goodenough, "The Perspective of Acts," in *Studies in Luke-Acts: Essays Presented in Honor of Paul Schubert*, ed. Leander E. Keck and J. Louis Martyn (Nashville: Abingdon, 1966; Philadelphia: Fortress Press, 1980) 55.

[6]Ibid., 56.

Paul's arrest by the Romans in Jerusalem and his being sent on to Rome—that
is, nearly the whole last quarter of Acts—can then have no claim to historicity
inasmuch as it all hangs upon Paul's claim to citizenship and his appeal to
Caesar.[7]

If all that part of Acts is fiction, including as it does so many accurate
topographical details and incidental references such as that of the ship "whose
sign was The Twin Brothers" (28:11) or to Publius as "the chief man" (Acts
28:7) of Malta,[8] then it is indeed a remarkable tour de force. The question would
necessarily arise whether the whole of Acts from 16:10 (when the first person
plural begins to be used) is not fiction. The result would be that the author of the
Third Gospel, who had shown such extreme care in giving the most accurate
account of the events there dealt with, had suddenly shown not only such a
difference of purpose but a profound difference of character. The preface to the
Gospel could hardly be called other than fraudulent.

Criticism must also be made of many of the statements in Haenchen's
monumental commentary. Haenchen has spoken of "him who knows how to read
between the lines and to hear what is left unsaid,"[9] but he often reads between
the lines to pour doubt on what is not there. In the essay from which those words
are taken Haenchen says of Acts 11:27-30: "At that time prophets from Jerusalem are reported to have walked to Antioch, a distance of 180 miles";[10] in fact
Acts says nothing of walking. More serious examples occur in Haenchen's
commentary. So, for example, in speaking of Paul's recovery from stoning at
Lystra, Haenchen writes: "On the very next day Paul is capable of resuming his
mission with full energy and vigor."[11] In fact, all Luke says is that after the
stoning "he rose up" (Acts 14:20) and that having managed to get up he left
Lystra the next day. Luke has nothing about suddenness or full vigor and energy.
Again in the account of the earthquake at Philippi, Haenchen regards "the
attempts to figure out how Paul could have seen through the opened door into
the lighted bedroom of the gaoler," as "both pathetic and comical,"[12] when in fact
Acts says that Paul addressed him not in his bedroom but when the gaoler saw

---

[7]Ibid.

[8]Cf. William M. Ramsay, *St. Paul the Traveller and the Roman Citizen,* 14th ed. enl.
(London: Hodder & Stoughton, 1920; [1]1895) 343: "The title 'first' is technically correct
in Melita [=Malta]: it has inscriptional authority."

[9]Ernst Haenchen, "The Book of Acts as Source Material for the History of Early
Christianity," in *Studies in Luke-Acts*, ed. Keck and Martyn, 261.

[10]Ibid., 269.

[11]Ernst Haenchen, *The Acts of the Apostles: A Commentary*, trans. Bernard Noble and
Gerald Shinn with Hugh Anderson and R. McL. Wilson (Oxford: Basil Blackwell;
Philadelphia: Westminster, 1971) 434.

[12]Ibid., 497n.8.

the prison doors open (Acts 16:27ff.). Ramsay's description[13] is truer to the text, and is the more natural explanation of the whole episode.

I take a further example: in dealing with Paul's arrest in the temple, Haenchen reads into Acts that "the almost fainting Paul was carried on the shoulders of the soldiers, where he was "completely exposed to every stone that is thrown,"[14] so that he could not have spoken to the crowd. But of course Luke does not say anything about "almost fainting" nor about the soldiers' shoulders, or for that matter about stone throwing. That Paul was "borne of the soldiers" (Acts 21:35) need mean no more than that he was carried along by them, as every television viewer has seen men "carried along" by the police; there is no suggestion in Acts that Paul was nearly fainting or incapable of making a speech.

Just as words in the speeches in Acts are sometimes put under a theological microscope whose use is quite inappropriate, its historical statements are sometimes subjected to a similar treatment. So, for example, on Acts 23:32 Haenchen cannot accept that "the infantry start their return march immediately,"[15] after marching from Jerusalem to Antipatris. But Luke is not chronicling the soldiers' history but Paul's. "On the morrow" the infantry drop out of the story, for it is the progress of the cavalry with Paul that matters. The infantry was left to return; just when they actually started out could hardly have interested Luke. He gives a broad outline of events, with the attention concentrated on what is relevant to his theme. This is not inconsistent with Lucan authorship.

It has been further argued against the conclusion that the author of Luke-Acts was a companion of Paul that Paul's teaching as represented in Acts is inconsistent with what is known from his letters. We have however to bear in mind both the difference between the purpose of the speeches in Acts and that of the epistles, and also the difference between the purpose of Paul as he is represented in the contexts of the speeches, in meeting different conditions and speaking to different audiences.

With regard to the first, the epistles give us examples of Paul's teaching addressed to Christians; the Acts (except in 20:18-35) gives an account of his preaching to the unconverted. The apostolic preaching was the proclamation of the saving acts of God in fulfillment of his promises to Israel; the teaching which followed drew out its implications. The true comparison is therefore between the records of preaching in Acts, and the indications of that preaching as they occur in the epistles. We may take, for example, what Paul himself says in Romans about the gospel he preached. The relevant passages are as follows:

> The gospel of God, which he promised afore by his prophets in the holy scriptures, concerning his Son, who was born of the seed of David according

---

[13]Ramsay, *St. Paul the Traveller*, 220-22.
[14]Haenchen, *Acts*, 618.
[15]Ibid., 650.

to the flesh, who was declared to be the Son of God with power, according to the spirit of holiness, by the resurrection of the dead; even Jesus Christ our Lord, through whom we have received grace and apostleship, unto obedience of faith among all the nations for his name's sake. —Rom 1:1-5

For I am not ashamed of the gospel, for it is the power of God unto salvation to every one that believeth, to the Jew first and also to the Greek. —Rom 1:16

The day when God shall judge the secrets of men, according to my gospel, by Jesus Christ. —Rom 2:16

If thou shalt confess with thy mouth Jesus as Lord, and shalt believe in thy heart that God raised him from the dead, thou shalt be saved. —Rom 10:9

According to my gospel and the preaching of Jesus Christ, according to the revelation of the mystery which hath been kept in silence through times eternal, but now is manifested, and by the scriptures of the prophets, according to the commandment of the eternal God, is made known unto all the nations unto obedience of faith. —Rom 16:25-26

In all these passages there is no single idea except that conveyed by the word "mystery" in the last quotation that is not paralleled in the Pauline speeches in Acts. Allowing for the fact that these can hardly be more than summaries of what Paul said, it does not appear that his preaching, as distinct from his teaching, was very different from what Acts describes.

Secondly, it is unrealistic to ignore the actual occasion of each of these speeches and the particular audience to which it was addressed. At Antioch (Acts 13:16-41), at Lystra (14:15-17), and at Athens (17:22-31) there were very different groups of hearers, and the speeches necessarily vary in their approach and contents. At Antioch Paul was in the synagogue, with a congregation consisting of Jews and devout converts to Judaism, and he could address them as "Men of Israel, and ye that fear God"; he could appeal to the history of Israel, to the Davidic origin of the Christ, and to the failure of the law as a means of justification. At Lystra, he was before a pagan population with the priest of Zeus prominent among them; he could only appeal to them to turn from paganism to a living God, and speak of the blessings they had received in their earthly lives in proof of his goodness. He had to start where people were. At Athens, before a more sophisticated urban population, a different approach was needed.

The speech of Paul at Athens has been much criticized, and held to show that the author of Acts compiled appropriate speeches to fit his scheme, but was not in a position to report what Paul actually said. For Conzelmann, for example, "The value of the description rests not in the historical worth of its details as sources of information about Paul's conduct, but in the fact that it documents for us how a Christian around A.D. 100 reacts to the *pagan* milieu and meets it from the position of his faith."[16] This ignores the fact that in Acts the effect of this method is shown to be a comparative failure, as is indeed implied by Paul in 1 Corinthians. It is of course a judgment that assumes a late date for Acts, and that it was not written by a companion of Paul.

If however there are solid grounds for believing Acts to be by Luke, the evidence for the reliability of the account in Acts should repay closer investigation. Too many assumptions are too easily made. According to Acts, while Paul was waiting at Athens (a phrase that rings true to fact; Paul was at Athens almost incidentally, having had to leave Beroea), he was provoked by evidences of idolatry (17:16). His first preaching was therefore not only "in the synagogue with the Jews and devout persons" as was his natural and inevitable custom (cf. Rom 2:9-10: "the Jew first and also the Greek") but also in argument in the Agora "with those who chanced to be there" (17:17 RSV; NEB and REB well translate "with casual passers-by"). There, according to Acts, he encountered some of the Epicurean and Stoic philosophers and also others, Athenians and foreigners, who were merely curious about novelties. This was not the heyday of Greek philosophy, nor was Athens then the undisputed cultural center of the world. We need not think of the philosophers whom Paul met as being of Socratic stature. Already, before the Areopagus speech, Paul was known to be speaking of Jesus and the Resurrection (17:18). It was as a result of the curiosity aroused by this that he was led to the Areopagus.

Conzelmann is probably correct in saying that the Areopagus here does not mean the court of that name, and that the events starting at 17:19 are not to be interpreted as a court trial. "The literary style of Luke rules that out: whenever he reports a trial he is absolutely unambiguous."[17] Whether Luke means Mars' Hill or some gathering of Areopagus members is open to question, but it is surely merely begging the question to say "Luke chooses the place not from his own geographical knowledge, but because of its historical reputation."[18] When Luke speaks first of the casual discussions in the Agora, it sounds like genuine reminiscence. At any rate, when Paul spoke, it was not to professional philosophers but to an Athenian crowd, perhaps not very different from that of other Hellenistic cities, but one with a veneer of philosophical culture. "It is significant," says Conzelmann, "that Luke, in spite of his philosophical audience does not start out from the monotheistic elements of contemporary philosophy (the Stoics), but from a subject of popular religion."[19] The audience may well have been more familiar with popular religion than with the monotheistic elements of Stoicism, as an English audience might be assumed to have a

---

[16]Hans Conzelmann, "The Address of Paul on the Areopagus," in *Studies in Luke-Acts*, ed. Keck and Martyn, 218.

[17]Conzelmann, "The Address of Paul on the Areopagus," 219.

[18]Ibid., 219-20.

[19]Ibid., 220.

superficial acquaintance with, say, the theory of evolution, without the audience consisting of professional scientists.

Much has been made of Paul's *captatio benevolentiae* (rather unfairly translated in the book containing Conzelmann's essay as "currying the audience's favor" or "the currying of favor."[20] It is a necessary element of oratory, except for those with a captive audience, and means "getting the goodwill" of the hearers, not necessarily to agreement with what is said, but to listen, "to give a hearing." Paul, who could say "I am become all things to all men, that I might by all means save some" (1 Cor 9:22), was quite capable of so beginning. Acts represents him as doing so in 24:10 and 26:2-3; the words of Rom 1:8ff. and 1 Cor 1:4ff. include much the same purpose. As reported in Acts, the speech at Athens is for the most part such a *captatio benevolentiae*. It would have had no chance of success if it had been couched in the language of Romans 1, but both deal with culpable ignorance. In the report of the speech, that only becomes clear when Paul proclaims that God now "commandeth men that they should all everywhere repent inasmuch as he hath appointed a day in the which he will judge the world in righteousness" (17:30-31). One does not need to repent of inculpable ignorance. It was when Paul came to the subjects of Judgment and the Resurrection that he lost the ear of most of his audience, some mocking, some saying "we will hear thee concerning this again" (17:32); only a few "clave unto him and believed." It is remarkable that if we want a summary of what Luke shows Paul to be aiming at, we find it in Paul's own words, written to those who "became an example to all the believers in Macedonia and Achaia": "how ye turned unto God from idols, to serve a living and true God, and to wait for his Son from heaven, whom he raised from the dead, even Jesus, which delivereth us from the wrath to come" (1 Thess 1:7-10). It was apparently the comparative failure to achieve this at Athens, where Paul seems to have been waiting hoping to return to Macedonia, that led to his going to Corinth where he became "occupied in preaching" (18:5 RSV). That he had learned by experience how not to reach Greek hearts is shown by what he says in 1 Cor 1:17-23.

We may notice from another speech of Paul in Acts a significant indication of Luke's faithful representation of Paul's preaching. In speaking to the elders of the church from Ephesus (Acts 20:28), Paul uses the phrase "the church of God which he purchased with his own blood." (The phrase could be translated rather differently, but the point is for our present purpose immaterial.) On this phrase Moule comments:

> Is it significant, then, that the one exception [namely, to the absence of any explicitly redemptive interpretation of the death of Christ] should be on the lips of Paul and in an address to an already Christian community? This is Paul, not some other speaker; and he is not evangelizing but recalling an already evan-

---

[20]*Studies in Luke-Acts,* ed. Keck and Martyn, 219, 213.

gelized community to its deepest insights. In other words, the situation, like the theology, is precisely that of a Pauline epistle, not of preliminary evangelism.[21]

It is an apt illustration of the necessary difference between Paul's first preaching and subsequent exhortations.

The factual accuracy of Luke in matters on which there is definite knowledge of the organization and practice in the Roman and Hellenistic world has been broadly vindicated (apart from the one unsolved problem of Quirinius in Luke 2:2), notably by Sherwin-White.[22] We are there in the realm of objective fact, and the facts are a confirmation of Luke's reliability as a reporter. His accuracy in such matters, which can be checked, is after all only in line with the scrupulous care that is to be seen in his dealing with matters he must have regarded as more important, and which can be illustrated at so many points in his Gospel.

Few ascriptions of authorship can have been subjected to such varied scrutinies as the traditional ascription of the Third Gospel to the "beloved physician," and from those scrutinies it emerges unscathed. If there are, as is often said, few assured results of New Testament criticism, this has a good claim to be one of them.

What the evidence gives us is not merely a name for the author but the assurance that his claim in the preface to the Gospel is true, that he had investigated what he was writing about; we can see his faithfulness to his sources, and that in writing Acts he had abundant access to reliable information. When he reports a speech it is no doubt "proved by its brevity to be rather the skeleton than the substance";[23] it is a precis, not a full report, but not the less reliable for that. When in the Gospel or Acts Luke selects from his materials it is in order to show the significance in relation to his overall plan. The theme of both volumes is the Gospel of Jesus—revealed in his life, death, and resurrection, and proclaimed according to his command. So the Gospel and Acts balance each other. As against Cadbury's conjecture "that the arrangement in Luke's Gospel of Jesus' prolonged progression to Jerusalem and death has been affected by the geographical character of Paul's career,"[24] we should hold that the progression of Acts reflects that of the Gospel. Events in Acts (Stephen's death for example) are seen in the light of events in the Gospel, not those of the Gospel in the light of Acts. They are part of the "fulfillment."

---

[21]C. F. D. Moule, "The Christology of Acts," in *Studies in Luke-Acts*, ed. Keck and Martyn, 171.

[22]A. N. Sherwin-White, *Roman Society and Roman Law in the New Testament,* The Sarum Lectures 1960–1961 (Oxford: Clarendon, 1963; rpt. 1965).

[23]Martin Dibelius, *From Tradition to Gospel,* trans. Bertram Lee Woolf (London: Ivor Robinson and Watson, 1934; New York: Scribner's, 1965; Greenwood SC: Attic, 1982) 25.

[24]Cadbury, *The Making of Luke-Acts,* 231-32.

The point at which Acts closes surely gives the most reliable clue to the date when Acts and therefore the Gospel were written. If Paul arrived in Rome in or about the year 60, and his unhindered preaching continued for two years, to A.D. 62, then whatever happened after that, the period during which his free preaching of the gospel in Rome can be set as the climax of the book lies between that date and the Neronian persecution. If we accept A.D. 65 as its date,[25] the completion of Acts must surely lie between those two dates, and that of the Gospel a little earlier than that of Acts. It is then, and then only, that the final words of Acts are the fitting end to Luke's two books.

---

[25]See Robinson, *Redating the New Testament,* 145ff.

Chapter 9

The Readers of the Gospel

Most excellent Theophilus . . . concerning the things wherein thou wast
instructed.   —Luke 1:3-4

In dedicating the Third Gospel and Acts to Theophilus Luke assumes
Theophilus has a vital interest in the matters dealt with, a concern to which he
has possibly given expression, but an interest and concern that are to be expected
in other readers also. To what sort of readers then does Luke address himself?

They are clearly people not of Palestine, but of the Roman world round the
Mediterranean. When Luke refers to the great cities of the Empire, he commonly
does so without explanation. This is true even of small places. There is something very matter-of-fact about passages such as "And when he met us at Assos,
we took him in, and came to Mitylene. And sailing from thence, we came the
following day over against Chios; and the next day we touched at Samos; and
the day after we came to Miletus" (Acts 20:14-15); or "And so we came to
Rome. And from thence the brethren, when they heard of us, came to meet us
as far as The Market of Appius, and The Three Taverns" (Acts 28:14-15).
Philippi, which would have a special interest for Luke if as appears he was left
there for a considerable time, is described as "a city of Macedonia, the first of
the district" and as a (Roman) colony; but so much description is exceptional.
Lystra and Derbe, as being more out of the beaten track, are described as "the
cities of Lycaonia" (Acts 14:5). Otherwise places are mentioned without such
comments.

References in the Gospel to places are very different. Jerusalem and Jericho
are mentioned without other explanation, but other places have some words of
explanation attached to their names. Mary lived at "a city of Galilee, named
Nazareth" (1:26); she went with Joseph "into Judæa, to the city of David, which
is called Bethlehem" (2:4); Capernaum was "a city of Galilee" (4:31); Jesus went
"to a city called Nain" (7:11); the country of the Gerasenes was "over against
Galilee" (8:26); Bethany and Bethphage were "at the mount called (the mount)
of Olives" (19:29); Arimathæa was "a city of the Jews" (23:51); there was "a
village named Emmaus, which was threescore furlongs from Jerusalem" (24:13).
It is the same with the topography of Jerusalem in Acts: "the mount called
Olivet, which is nigh unto Jerusalem, a sabbath day's journey off" (1:12); "the

door of the temple which is called Beautiful" (3:2); "the porch that is called Solomon's" (3:11), which afterwards can be referred to simply as "Solomon's porch" (5:12). What is clear is that Luke does not expect his readers to have much local knowledge.

It is part of the thesis of Conzelmann in his study of Luke's theology[1] that Luke uses particular kinds of territory (mountain, plain, desert, lake) for symbolic reasons, and that "his acquaintance with Palestine is in many respects imperfect." For example, he writes, "It is true that according to Luke Jesus does in fact come to Jericho, but it is questionable whether Luke knew that this town was in the region of the Jordan."[2] What in fact we know is that Luke in the parable of the Good Samaritan speaks of a man "going down from Jerusalem to Jericho" (10:30) and later, after Jesus had been at Jericho, of his "going up to Jerusalem" (19:28), both of which statements are geographically accurate. For that matter, the dangers of the road, described in the parable, are true to reality. So elsewhere Conzelmann writes (on Luke 4:31-44): "It is of course geographically correct to say that Jesus comes 'down' to Capernaum, but this does not necessarily imply an accurate geographical knowledge on Luke's part. Κατά might well be deduced from the incorrect idea that Nazareth stands on a hill."[3] Of course it might, but there is no reason to assume it. Luke must have known that Capernaum was by the lake, and if, as I hold, he knew Matthew, he could even have found "Capernaum by the sea" given as a description (Matt 4:13) in the very sentence from which he took the unusual form "Nazara" for Nazareth. Luke may never have visited Nazareth or Capernaum, but he shows a true picture of the general geography of the Holy Land. The acquaintance of anyone with any country is "imperfect" but there is no reason to think that Luke's knowledge of Palestine was incorrect.

According to Conzelmann,

> Most remarkable of all . . . is the fact that we are not told anywhere in Luke that Capernaum is situated by the lake. Yet the fact that it is situated here is part and parcel of many of the traditions. . . . If one were not familiar with Mark, one would have the impression that Capernaum was in the middle of Galilee. Is that Luke's idea, thinking that Jesus would not choose as his center a place at the edge of this region?[4]

---

[1]Hans Conzelmann, "Geographical Elements in the Composition of Luke's Gospel," *The Theology of St. Luke,* trans. Geoffrey Buswell (London: Faber and Faber, 1960; New York: Harper, 1961; Philadelphia: Fortress, 1982).

[2]Ibid., 19.

[3]Ibid., 38-39.

[4]Ibid., 39.

The difficulty is imaginary. Luke has already said that Simon's house was at Capernaum (4:38); in 5:1-11 he shows that Simon was a fisherman at the lake; the connection is surely obvious.

Another example of a forced interpretation that Conzelmann makes of Luke's geographical references concerns John the Baptist. On the words of Luke 3:3—"And he came into all the region round about Jordan"—Conzelmann comments that it

> suggests the idea of itinerant preaching, and all the more so, in that it has no support in the parallel passages. It is true that Matthew makes a statement which seems very similar, but it has in fact a characteristic difference: all the region round about Jordan comes to him. Matthew therefore presupposes a fixed locality by the Jordan, as Matt 3:6 shows.[5]

In fact Mark 1:4 has that John "baptized in the wilderness," and more to the point Matt 3:1 has John "preaching in the wilderness of Judæa." Like Matthew and Mark, Luke records that the baptism of Jesus was in the Jordan (4:1), but his statement that John was also to be found "in all the region round about Jordan, preaching the baptism of repentance" receives very specific confirmation in John 3:23: "And John also was baptizing in Aenon near to Salim, because there was much water [Greek: were many waters] there; and they came and were baptized." It is not the only case where Luke and John show knowledge of traditions not reflected in Matthew or Mark.

A more important point to Conzelmann is that he interprets Luke as imagining "that Judæa and Galilee are immediately adjacent, and that Samaria lies alongside them, apparently bordering on both the regions."[6] The argument has been adequately answered in Marshall's *Luke, Historian and Theologian,* and with it the conclusions that Conzelmann derives from his theory. "There is . . . nothing strange," writes Marshall,

> in Luke's use of the geographical terminology, once it is recognized that Judæa has both a broad and a narrow meaning. Conzelmann's picture of Jesus moving to and fro across an imaginary Judæan-Galilean frontier proves to be an illusion. Rather Luke uses "Judæa" as a term which includes Galilee, and the reason for this usage (which has involved him in altering his Marcan source at Luke 4:44) may lie in the fact that he does not ascribe theological importance to Galilee; it is the place where the gospel "begins" (Acts 10:37) but not its main theater.[7]

---

[5]Ibid., 19.

[6]Ibid., 69.

[7]I. Howard Marshall, *Luke, Historian and Theologian,* Contemporary Evangelical Perspectives (Exeter: Paternoster Press, 1970; Grand Rapids MI: Zondervan, 1971) 71.

The only qualification I would make to this is in demurring from the assumption that Luke was altering a "Marcan source."

Conzelmann's theories about Lucan geography depend on the assumption that the author was not the companion of Paul, himself having been at Jerusalem (Acts 21:15-17). But even apart from the evidence of authorship by that companion, the statements of Luke and Acts do not justify Conzelmann's conclusions. Luke may well have seen a symbolic fitness in, for example, Jesus going into the hills to pray (6:12; 9:28), but such considerations do not involve any suggestion that he did not believe he was recording facts, or that his knowledge of the country was inadequate.

Luke then supplies his readers with sufficient information of the context of Jesus' life for the purpose of the gospel, but he does not assume that they are themselves acquainted with the territory of Palestine.

With regard to the Jewish background of the life of Jesus, a distinction has to be made. A good deal of knowledge of the religion of Israel, such as could be had from acquaintance with the Old Testament, is taken for granted. Local religious customs and practice are not expected to be understood, nor are they relevant to the needs of his readers. It is clear from the beginning of the Gospel that some knowledge may be assumed. Zacharias executed the priest's office in "the temple of the Lord" (1:8-9), and it is not necessary to say that this was at Jerusalem. Zacharias's wife was "of the daughters of Aaron" (1:5), and the expression is not thought to need explanation. Jesus was given his name "when eight days were fulfilled for circumcising him" (1:21), and was taken to the temple "when the days of their purification according to the law of Moses were fulfilled" (2:22), and an acquaintance with the Old Testament scriptures gives the reader sufficient background knowledge to appreciate what is referred to. References to Elijah and Elisha (4:25-27) would be clear to such readers, as would that to "the city of David" (2:4). The Christians of the empire, for whom Luke wrote, would include not only Jews, but others who "feared God" (cf. Acts 13:16, 26), who had some connection with the synagogue, and converted Gentiles who with the rest of the church came to accept the Old Testament as Scripture.

On the other hand there were many elements in contemporary Palestinian life that were of no significance to Luke's readers, though they are frequently mentioned in Matthew. When Mark (7:1ff.) uses such material from Matthew he adds his own explanation (7:3-4); Luke avoids such material. The Pharisees could not be ignored, though instead of "they make broad their phylacteries, and enlarge the borders" (Matt 23:5), it was more understandable to say they "desire to walk in long robes" (20:46); but the Sadducees could generally be ignored. Luke only refers to them in two connections: he has to do so in 20:27 and in Acts 23:6-8 because they were those who said "there is no resurrection"; and again in Acts 4:1 and 5:17 because they were associated with the high priest's party, and indeed at Acts 4:1 because it was also a matter of "the resurrection from the dead." Otherwise, Luke need not complicate his narrative with them.

The scribes also could not be left out of the account, but it is noticeable that when he first mentions them (5:17; also Acts 5:34) it is as νομοδιδάσκαλοι, "doctors (RSV teachers) of the law," a word not used by Matthew; and he also uses the word νομικός, "lawyer," on seven occasions, one of them (10:25) being from Matthew (22:35).

The term "rabbi" never occurs in Luke; like Matthew (23:7) he speaks of those who love "the salutations in the marketplaces" (11:43; 20:46), but he omits Matthew's continuation "and to be called of men, Rabbi." Luke clearly prefers to use Greek words for his Greek-speaking readers. The characteristic phrase on Jesus' lips, "Amen I say unto you," represented in all four Gospels, occurs only six times in Luke, as against five times that number in Matthew. Of the six times in Luke, three of them (18:17; 18:29; 21:32) are taken from Matthew; three are without Matthaean parallels. More frequently Luke reduces the phrase to "I say unto you." As against the parallel in Matt 24:27, Luke 12:44 has "of a truth (ἀληθῶς) I say unto you"; as against Matt 3:36, Luke at 11:51 has "Yea (ναί) I say unto you." The passage in Matthew where Jesus cried with a loud voice (27:46-49) saying "Eli, Eli, lama sabachthani?" has no parallel in Luke. Gethsemane simply becomes "the place" (22:40); Golgotha "the place which is called the Skull" (23:33).

The same change from a Palestinian outlook can be observed in the simple fact that whereas Matthew regularly speaks of "the kingdom of heaven," or more literally "the kingdom of the heavens," Luke regularly alters this to "the kingdom of God." Matthew also regularly has "the heavens" in the plural, Luke "heaven" in the singular. There is one surprising exception, when Matt 6:20 has "treasures in heaven" and Luke 12:33 has "treasure in the heavens."

Many of Luke's omissions from Matthew are due to their Palestinian connections. So in the Sermon on the Mount, the passages on almsgiving, prayer, and fasting, the criticisms of those who sound a trumpet before them in the synagogues and in the streets, or who love to pray in the synagogues and in the corners of the streets, or who "disfigure their faces that they may be seen unto men to fast" (Matt 6:2-10), were not likely to seem relevant to the readers in the empire. The illustrations of the way the righteousness of Christian disciples must exceed the righteousness of the scribes and Pharisee, which Matthew includes in the same Sermon, are understandably omitted by Luke. So also is a good deal of the material in the woes against the Pharisees (Matt 23:1-26), which reflects conditions foreign to Luke's readers.

So far we have been dealing with things Luke's readers might be expected not to be concerned about. How then does Luke meet their actual needs? The first answer is very simple, though it sometimes seems to be forgotten in discussions of Luke's theology. The readers needed to know what were the actual facts about Jesus, what he had done and what he had taught, and that their faith was built on a sure foundation.[8] Only so could they be sure of the validity of the instruction they had been given. That he has gone to pains to provide this is the claim Luke makes in the preface to his Gospel. His integrity can be seen where he is closely following Matthew as his sole source in relating the words of Jesus, or where he is at pains to avoid giving a wrong context when he alters the position of one of Matthew's episodes. In spite of the frequently made assumption that Luke felt free to invent suitable speeches in Acts, the evidence is surely against this.

Apart from the natural desire of Christians to know more of the events of the life of Jesus and of his teaching, there were inevitably matters of special concern. To a church whose membership included converted Jews, God-fearers, and pagans, one such concern was the relationship of Christianity to the old Israel. The Gospel had come out of a Jewish milieu, but obviously was rejected by many Jews and by their leaders. It had therefore to be shown that Jesus was not only an authentic son of Israel, but was the one in whom the true vocation of Israel had been fulfilled. It was necessary to show that not only was the Gospel valid though rejected by most of Israel, but that in his own lifetime Jesus stood vindicated when he himself was rejected, and that rejection was itself part of the fulfillment of the prophecies of the old Scriptures.

The main theme of Luke's introductory chapters (1–4) then is the proclamation of Jesus as the promised Messiah and the destined Son of David. The atmosphere of Jewish piety pervades these chapters, from the first mention of Zacharias and Elisabeth "walking in all the commandments and ordinances of the Lord blameless" (1:6); and Jesus is shown as brought up in this environment. That he is the Christ is the underlying theme. So when John the precursor (1:17) is the subject of people's questioning "whether haply he were the Christ" (3:15) he points to one who is coming,[9] clearly meant to be understood by Luke's readers as Jesus. It is when the claim that Jesus is a true son of Israel, the Christ and the Son of David, has been made clear, that Luke can proceed to tell the story "beginning from Galilee, after the baptism which John preached; how that God anointed Jesus of Nazareth with the Holy Spirit and with power, who went about doing good, and healing all that were oppressed by the devil" (Acts 10:37-38).

The crowning episode of Luke's introduction was the baptism of Jesus, when the voice from heaven declared him God's beloved Son, and the Holy Spirit came upon him. Luke keeps this before his readers: whereas Matthew simply has

---

[8]Cf. Helmut Flender, *St. Luke: Theologian of Redemptive History*, trans. Reginald H. Fuller and Ilse Fuller (London; Philadelphia: Fortress, 1967) 46.

[9]In spite of 1:17, to which he refers, Conzelmann (*The Theology of St. Luke,* 24-25) says "John is not the precursor, for there is no such thing"—that is, according to Conzelmann, in Luke's view. It seems significant to Conzelmann that Luke 3:16 "omits ὀπίσω μου"; but Acts 13:25 has μετ᾽ ἐμέ with the same meaning. Luke's variation is merely stylistic.

"Then was Jesus led up of the Spirit to be tempted of the devil" (4:1), Luke expands this to "And Jesus, full of the Holy Spirit, returned from the Jordan, and was led by the Spirit in the wilderness" (4:1). The Temptation that follows would be meaningless apart from Jesus being the Messiah: the first of the three temptations depends on the words "If thou art the Son of God"; in the second, authority over the kingdoms of the world implies the same messianic consciousness in Jesus; and the third repeats the words "If thou art the Son of God." And as the Spirit has led Jesus in the wilderness, so for Matthew's words "he withdrew into Galilee" (4:12) Luke writes "Jesus returned in the power of the Spirit into Galilee" (4:14). The reader is prepared for the programmatic sermon at Nazareth, with its text "the Spirit of the Lord is upon me, because he anointed me" (4:18). It is in the light of the claim that now this scripture has been fulfilled, with the exposition of the works of the Messiah, that the story of the Ministry continues. It is to these works that Jesus appeals, when the disciples of John come to question him (7:22-23).

At his trial Jesus is challenged: "If thou art the Son of God, tell us" (22:67), and it is as a result of the charge that he said "that he himself is Christ a king" (23:2) that he went to his death. If it is true, as has been said, that Luke has no deep *theologia crucis,* the outstanding point in his Gospel is still that Jesus' claim to be the Christ and Savior, although his Crucifixion was "unto Jews a stumbling-block and unto Gentiles foolishness" (1 Cor 1:23), is vindicated in two ways. It is vindicated by the revelation of his Resurrection and Ascension (the point from which Luke's second volume is to develop its theme), and by the demonstration of what is put into the lips of Jesus in the Resurrection stories, that it behooved the Christ to suffer and so to enter his glory (24:7, 26, 46). "The things fulfilled among us" carry their own justification: "History, for Luke, has brought the prophecies to fulfillment, and the prophecies prove that the historical events happened according to the will of God."[10]

But the gospel was still rejected by the bulk of the Jews. So a further thread, that of rejection, runs through the Gospel. Already in the story of the presentation in the temple there is the warning that Jesus was "set for the falling and rising up of many in Israel, and for a sign which is spoken against" (2:34). The very sermon at Nazareth that opens the proclamation of the good news in the Ministry was the occasion when in his own hometown men "rose up and cast him forth out of the city" (4:28), a grim foreshadowing of what was to happen at Jerusalem.

Those who hold to the hypothesis of Mark's priority commonly raise the question whether the conflict stories found in Mark 2:1–3:6 (parallel to Luke

---

[10]Nils A. Dahl, "The Story of Abraham in Luke-Acts," in *Studies in Luke-Acts,* trans. Leander E. Keck and J. Louis Martyn (Nashville: Abingdon, 1966; Philadelphia: Fortress, 1980) 153.

5:17–6:11, and to the two groups in Matt 9:1-17, 12:1-14) once formed a
separate collection. "It is possible," wrote Nineham,

> that these five stories formed a collection before they reached their present
> position in this Gospel [namely, Mark]. . . . We find a constant if indirect
> emphasis by Jesus himself on his office and its purpose ([Mark] 2:10, 17, 28),
> and the shadow of the final Passion is already present (2:19-20; 3:6).[11]

If the case that has already been argued in the present book is valid, it is Luke
who has united two groups of material from Matthew (and has been followed by
Mark in doing so), extending into the Galilean Ministry the theme of opposition,
which he has previously begun to illustrate.

Rejection of God's word was not a new feature in Israel's history, as Jesus
says in the Sermon on the Mount in Matthew (6:23); Luke includes the same reference, though he follows what is probably a different tradition of the form of
the Beatitudes: "Blessed are you when men hate you, and when they ostracize
you and revile you, and cast out your name as evil, for the Son of man's sake
. . . for in the same way did their fathers do to the prophets" (6:22-23). It is not
necessarily a prophecy of persecution by state action, but of the kind of situation
referred to in 1 Thess 1:14: "Ye also suffered the same things of your own coun-
trymen as they [namely, the churches of God in Judæa] did of the Jews"; or in
2 Thess 1:4: "in all the persecutions and in all the afflictions which ye endure."
Whether among Jews or Gentiles, rejection and reviling were to be expected.

Persecution for the name of Christ is predicted again in Luke 21:12ff. The
parallel passage in Matthew (10:17ff.) may reflect a more Jewish background, as
Luke omits "they will flog you in their synagogues," an affliction to which most
of his readers could not be subject,[12] but probably Luke is only abbreviating
slightly. Acts gives instances of Christians being brought "before kings and
governors" as Jesus himself had been brought before Herod and Pilate, himself
fulfilling what God's hand and counsel "foreordained to come to pass" (Acts
4:25-28).

As to the leaders of the Jewish nation, the death of Jesus is shown to be the
result of the exertions of "the chief priests and scribes" who sought his death
(Luke 22:2) and of those who were led by them. It was "the chief priests and the
rulers of the people" whom Pilate called together (23:12), and who cried out for
Jesus' crucifixion. Alone among the evangelists Luke shows that there were those
among the people who were distressed at his death: "women who bewailed and
lamented him" (23:27); the "great multitude of the people" who also followed
him to Calvary (23:27) and who "stood beholding" (23:35) until they returned

---

[11]Dennis E. Nineham, *The Gospel of St. Mark*, Pelican Gospel Commentaries
(Baltimore: Penguin Books, 1963; New York: Seabury Press, 1968) = *St. Mark*,
Westminster Pelican Commentaries (Philadelphia: Westminster Press, 1978) 89.

[12]But cf. 2 Cor 11:24 as concerning Jewish Christians.

"smiting their breasts" (23:48). The division to be seen later among the Jews of the empire was already to be seen among those of Palestine in Jesus' own day. It was to be expected, it was in line with their history, it was foretold; it was no argument against belief in him.

But if Jesus was the true Messiah of Israel, even though most of Israel rejected him, what was the place of the Gentiles in God's plan? Already at the beginning of the Gospel Luke gives intimations of their acceptance: Simeon proclaims Jesus as "a light for revelation to the Gentiles" as well as "the glory of God's people Israel" (2:32); the quotation from Isaiah applied by Matthew to the Baptist is extended to include "all flesh shall see the salvation of God" (3:6); the genealogy is carried back through David and Abraham to "Adam, the son of God" (3:38). The story of the healing of the centurion's servant, which as in Matthew follows the Great Sermon, evokes from Jesus the words "I have not found so great faith, no not in Israel" (7:9), and the commendation of the centurion in 7:4 (not included in Matthew) suggests that Luke may well have connected this episode in his mind with the story of another centurion, Cornelius, in Acts 10, commended for his alms and prayers, whose faith first broke the barrier to the reception of Gentiles into the Church. The words that Matthew includes in his own account (probably inserting 8:11-12 into his narrative from a different source, as is suggested by the introduction "And I say unto you" of those "who shall come from the east and west, and from the north and south, and shall sit down in the kingdom of God" appear in Luke in the wider context raised by the question "Are there few that be saved?" (13:22-30). Shortly after, the same lesson is repeated in the parable of the Great Supper, with the command to "go out into the highways and hedges" (14:15-24). The final resurrection appearance recorded by Luke includes, in the words of the risen Lord, as part of what is written in the Old Testament scriptures, "that repentance and remission of sins should be preached in his name unto all the nations, beginning from Jerusalem" (24:47). It is to show that this part of God's purpose, foretold in the Scriptures, was one of the things fulfilled, that the Acts of the Apostles was written. When the Gospel was being preached in Rome, the symbol of the Gentile nations, the theme of Luke is completed.

Luke's readers, however, were not only concerned with their relation to Israel; and dealing with the attitude of the Jewish authorities, whether in the Gospel or Acts, inevitably raised the question of relationship to the Roman power. The Christians of the period up to Nero's persecution were already in a potentially dangerous situation. Warnings such as those of Rom 13:1-7. Titus 3:1 and 1 Pet 2:13, 17 (if they all come from this period) were very relevant. Luke does not go in for exhortations, but he, like Matthew, includes the command to render to Caesar the things that are Caesar's (20:25). What he does seek to show, both in recording the trial of Jesus and the story of Paul, is that the Christian Way has not been condemned by Rome. In the trial of Jesus, Pilate on three occasions is recorded as pronouncing Jesus innocent (23:4, 15, 22), in each case in words without parallel in Matthew, or for that matter in Mark; John 18:38 has one such declaration. The Roman centurion at the Crucifixion bore the same testimony (23:47). So later, in Acts, Luke records that Peter could claim that it was Jews who had denied Jesus "before the face of Pilate, when he was determined to release him" (Acts 3:13). Pilate's miscarriage of justice did not imply a condemnation of Jesus by Roman law.

What could be claimed for Jesus could be claimed also for his followers: on no occasion had it happened that they had been found guilty before the Roman law on account of their religion. Of the attacks on Paul and his companions which are recorded in Acts, two (those at Philippi and Ephesus) are not laid to the charge of Jews; at Corinth, a definite allegation was made by Jews that Christians were breaking the Roman law, but this was dismissed; elsewhere, at Antioch in Pisidia (Acts 13:50), Iconium (14:5), Lystra (14:19), Thessalonica (17:5), and Beroea (17:13), persecutions began through Jewish instigations though the repeated references to "the multitudes" and at Thessalonica to "wicked fellows of the rabble" show, not for the first time or the last in history, how mob violence can take over. Luke was writing for people who might well experience such violence.

The last scenes of Acts concern the trial of Paul himself and its consequences. It was to escape being tried at Jerusalem that Paul appealed to Caesar (29:9-12), and his appeal was based on the expectation of being acquitted. After the hearing before Agrippa, Festus was told that "this man might have been set at liberty, if he had not appealed to Caesar" (26:32). Acts then closes with Paul, still presumably confident of acquittal, preaching at Rome without hindrance. The shadow of official Roman persecution had yet to fall on the Church.

Luke was writing for people who in an uncertain world were aware of the hostility of the Jews, and no doubt of the suspicion of many others among whom they lived, and of the danger of arousing the hostility of the Roman power. Their constancy depended on the assurance of the truth of salvation through Christ, and that they were within the sphere of that salvation, It has been well said that

> the central theme in the writings of Luke is that Jesus Christ offers salvation to men. If we were looking for a text to sum up the message of the Gospel, it would undoubtedly be Luke 19:10: "For the Son of man came to seek and to save the lost."[13]

To strengthen the faith of his readers, Luke had a two-fold task: to show Jesus as the Savior and to show that it was God's will that salvation was offered to all, Jew or Gentile. He fulfilled the first task in the Gospel, the second in the Acts.

Luke might have said, in the words that John's Gospel records, "salvation is of the Jews" (John 4:20). It is at Jerusalem, the heart of Jewry, that Luke's Gospel begins, with the thought of God as the Savior of Israel. So Mary in the

---

[13]Marshall, *Luke, Historian and Theologian,* 116.

Magnificat speaks of God her Savior who remembered mercy "toward Abraham and his seed" (1:47, 55); Zacharias spoke of his son's calling to prepare the way of the Lord "to give knowledge of salvation unto his people" (1:77); and the message of the angel at Jesus' birth was of a Savior whose coming was good news to "all the people"—and "Abraham's seed" and "the people" mean the people of Israel. Salvation could even be described as "the redemption of Jerusalem" (2:38). Luke makes it very clear that salvation is "from the Jews"; it was among the Jews that it was first proclaimed. That is where Luke begins; he closes with the declaration "this salvation of God is sent unto the Gentiles" (Acts 28:28).

It was of this salvation that Luke was writing for his contemporaries in the empire. There are important implications of this for the understanding of Lucan theology. What Luke wrote was a justification of the Christian gospel for the converts of his time. He might well have called his two volumes by a common title—"The Christian Kerygma, volumes 1 and 2" or "God's Purpose Fulfilled, parts 1 and 2"—for the whole scope of the kerygma, from the birth of Jesus to the apostolic witness to the Gentiles, was his subject. He was not writing one volume as a "Gospel" and another as the first "History of the Christian Church" for others to add to through future ages.

This simple fact is important for the understanding of Lucan theology, especially in the field of eschatology. Luke was a faithful transmitter of the tradition he had received, not a theological innovator. In particular he was not abandoning or reshaping eschatology, "historicizing" the story of Jesus and the gospel, or seeing the days of Jesus as "the middle of time," if that means that he must have thought of the Parousia of Jesus as in the remote future. When he thought it might be, or if he even asked himself the question, is certainly something we do not know; he may have expected it in his own lifetime. What he was showing was that the witness to the Gentiles completed the list of items in the apostolic tradition, all of which had to precede the End.

In the course of carrying out his task, Luke recorded as accurately as he could what the tradition included of the predictions of Jesus. They were in fact of four kinds, dealing with his own death and resurrection, the destruction of Jerusalem, the future persecution of his disciples, and the close of the Age. It is not always easy to distinguish in the accounts of these in the Gospels what the tradition itself had not always kept distinct. What Luke certainly did was to transmit a faithful account of what had been handed down in his sources.

There is a link between all these predictions, for they all concern aspects of one great process: they are all "eschatological." The forces of evil which Jesus was challenging would bring about his death, and the same forces would still operate to cause in turn the persecution of his disciples. Before the end comes "they shall lay their hands on you, and shall persecute you . . . for my name's sake" (21:12). Such forces would pursue their blind course, and one inevitable result would be the destruction of Jerusalem, which did not know the things that belonged to its peace. On the other hand, Jesus was confident of his vindication.

When Luke wrote, he could speak of the Resurrection and Ascension as the inauguration of the reign of Christ, and he could look forward to the final coming in glory as the crowning manifestation of his lordship.

More clearly than Matthew, Luke points to the identity between the conditions that brought about Jesus' death and those that would result in the destruction of Jerusalem. This is illustrated by the words of Jesus' lament over Jerusalem (19:41-44) and by the episode on the way to Calvary where Jesus addresses the "daughters of Jerusalem" (23:28-31)—the form of address is itself significant. Neither of these passages is paralleled in Matthew. Predictions of the destruction of Jerusalem are conflated by Matthew in his apocalyptic discourse in chapter 24, and Luke follows him in this,[14] but Luke omits Matt 24:26-28, 37-41, for which he has an independent and fuller tradition that he records elsewhere (17:22-37); and Matt 24:42-51, which Luke follows closely in wording but includes in his general teaching section, introduced by a passage that has parallels with Matthew's connected parable of the Ten Virgins (Matt 25:1-13) at Luke 12:35-46.

Luke is clearly faithful to his sources, and in being so, goes to some extent behind Matthew's conflations; but there is no sign that he has intended to reinterpret the tradition. He does not doubt that signs in the sun and moon and stars will precede the coming of the Son of man in a cloud with power and great glory, when the faithful can look up and know that "redemption draweth nigh." The Parousia is still real for him, but his primary interest is in the reassurance of the converts of the empire, now that the gospel has been brought to them, and the program of the apostolic mission is in principle completed. It was to show that this was so that Luke needed his second volume.

---

[14]The difference in outlook between Matthew and Luke is illustrated by Matt 24:15—"When therefore ye see the abomination of desolation . . . in the holy place"—and Luke 2:20-22. To Luke "all things which are written" are to be fulfilled, but he concentrates on "Jerusalem compassed with armies," not on the desecration of the temple.

Conclusion

With a collection of material, including the First Gospel, at his disposal, and with a wider readership in mind, Luke put his hand to writing. He had first to portray Jesus as the Savior. In his three introductory chapters the coming of Jesus as Savior is heralded and ratified by the divine voice "This is my Son" at the Baptism.

Already in these chapters there are indications of the universal significance of that coming, but they are no more than that since the Gospel must speak of the proclamation of the Kingdom in Israel. From this point the meaning of salvation has to be illustrated and revealed through the deeds and words of Jesus. So after rejecting the temptations to a false messiahship Jesus is shown at Nazareth announcing that the day has come for the blessings of salvation foretold by Isaiah to be fulfilled. After that, he is seen as the Savior in action: healing the sick, casting out demons, cleansing the leper, declaring the forgiveness of sins, and preaching the good news to the poor.

Then the coming of John's messengers gives Jesus the opportunity to appeal to what has happened as revealing the nature of his mission. After this the story is continued until Jesus makes the challenge to his immediate disciples: "Who say ye that I am?" and receives their answer in Peter's words: "The Christ of God." Now Jesus can begin to prepare them for the thought of his death and resurrection, and of his final coming in glory.

So the witness about the deeds of Jesus ("all that Jesus began to do") itself culminates in the Transfiguration, which in Luke's Gospel both looks back to what has been revealed ("This is my Son") and looks forward to what is to happen ("the exodus which he was about to accomplish at Jerusalem"), and to the meaning of his teaching ("Hear ye him"), which Luke was to record before that "exodus."

In what follows, Luke keeps before the mind of his readers that the goal of all Jesus' journeyings is Jerusalem. The Christ is going to the scene of his death and resurrection. With his reminders that Jesus himself was on the way to Jerusalem, Luke includes and indeed begins with the instruction of his disciples as they are being prepared for their future mission. Jesus warns them of the claims of discipleship; he prepares them for the trials ahead of them; he predicts the strains that discipleship will bring and the cost it will demand. The theme of salvation, and of the bringing of the gospel of salvation, runs through the whole section: "And they shall come from the east and west, and from the north and south, and shall sit down in the kingdom of God" (13:29); "Go out into the highways and hedges and constrain them to come in" (14:23); "I have found my sheep which was lost" (15:6); "thy brother was dead and is alive again, and was lost and is found" (15:32); "the Son of man came to seek and to save that which was lost" (19:10).

In the account of Jesus' teaching, the presence of opposition, already shown in the earlier part of the Gospel, is repeatedly referred to. The disciples will meet with rejection, as Jesus himself did (10:16); he was himself accused of casting out demons through the prince of demons (11:14-20); he had to denounce the hypocrisy of the Pharisees and lawyers, and aroused their hatred (11:37-54; 15:2); as they had not learned from Moses and the prophets, they would not be persuaded though one rose from the dead (16:31).

Luke therefore gradually prepares for the story of the Passion, and for the interpretation of its place in the divine purpose which recurs in his account of the Resurrection appearances. It is already summarized in the quotation from Psalm 118:22: "The stone which the builders rejected, the same was made the head of the corner" (20:17). Luke's readers were to see the hand of God in Christ's passion and death, and to see his vindication in the Resurrection. Then the Gospel comes to a rapid close with the reference to the Ascension, which was to be the starting point for the second of Luke's volumes. It was left to that to show how the rest of God's promises for man's salvation were to be fulfilled, as all flesh would see the salvation of God, and Jesus would be a light for revelation to the Gentiles.

Jesus was taken into heaven, and the Gospel ends, leaving the disciples where the whole story began, in the temple at Jerusalem, rejoicing at Jesus' triumph (24:32-52).

* * *

I close with a little picture—imaginary, but I think not far from the truth. It shows a man with a pen poised ready to write. Clearly a cultured person, actually a physician by profession. A man of deep compassion, with a great concern for those in trouble: the poor, the sick, the widowed, the distressed. A devout man, attracted first by the religion of the Jews, until he found its fulfillment in the good news of Jesus the Messiah.

That was the great turning point in his life, and it had led to another. He had crossed the path of the great man who was to become his hero, whose name was Paul. So he became one of Paul's team of helpers, and with them he had seen men and cities, and had helped to form the little Christian communities scattered round the Mediterranean.

A studious person, he had collected all he could of information about the deeds and words of Jesus. Then came another turning point: he came to know a book that was being circulated in the Christian churches; future generations were to call it Matthew's Gospel. It was very good, admirable for those for whom it had been compiled, but perhaps not quite what would best suit the little groups he knew so well, at places like Philippi and Corinth and Ephesus. Now he had written a book himself, with their special needs and circumstances in mind, omitting what was less appropriate, adding from his own collection. He would follow it later with a second volume, showing how the good news had come to the whole Empire.

So now he had finished his first book. There was one sentence to add, the last he would write, but the first to be read: a dedication, in the appropriate formal style, to an honored friend. He put his pen to the parchment and began: "Forasmuch as many have taken in hand. . . . "

Index of Authors